GETTING AFRICA OUT OF THE DUNGEON: HUMAN RIGHTS, FEDERALISM, AND JUDICIAL POLITICS IN CAMEROON

By

Peter Ateh-Afac Fossungu

AFRICA TALENT PUBLISHERS (PVT) LTD
... home to Africa's finest talent

Masvingo, Zimbabwe

i

Africa Talent Publishers

15155

Runyararo West

Masvingo, Zimbabwe

Email: mmawere@atpublishers.co.zw

tmubaya@atpublishers.co.zw

Tel:+263 776 966 915/+263 772 973 019

Website: http://www.atpublishers.co.zw/

ISBN: 9780797497818

DEDICATED TO DEAR SWEET MAMA AFRICA

CONTENTS

Introduction

This book focuses squarely on the judiciary as, first, the third branch of government, second, the acknowledged umpire of federalism and, finally, an exquisite means of reversing the institutionalization of inhuman rights and injustice administration in Cameroon – Africa's supposed legendary pathfinder: viewing President Amadou Ahidjo's claims in 1961 that the new Cameroon state was to be a real laboratory for an African Union, bringing together all the English-speaking and French-speaking countries of the continent (Fossungu, 2013a: viii). The prevailing and unsettling human rights situation in African countries like Cameroon cannot then fail to attract keen attention to the judiciary and its independence as well as to the concept of federalism which, according to some experts, is "a device which I find to be the best or authentic modern vehicle for multiculturalism or the political management of ethnic/cultural diversity" (Fossungu, 2013b: x). Cameroonians from all the corners of the country as well as all those interested in what is going on in this unique African country (singular in being the only that is variously known as 'Africa in Miniature', 'Africa's Promised Land', 'Paradise in Africa', 'the hinge of Africa', 'the microcosm of Africa' (Fossungu, 2013a: vii)) are entitled to understand what the problem actually is and what would need to be done to permanently redress it. That is the reason I have taken the time to bring forth this revised and updated version of *some portions* of my close to 500-page 1999 doctoral dissertation at the Université de Montréal. It comes to throw shining light on the roots and causes of the quagmire, as well as advance some means of resolving the human rights and justice administration problems bisecting not only this nation but also the continent generally. The hope is that this contribution would provide enhanced understanding of what is currently happening in Cameroon and Africa at large and, perhaps, bring about a rethinking of neo-colonial government's out-of-touch policy on biculturalism and national development.

But the contribution has not come to simply beg for the administration's rethinking. It comes instead to show Cameroonians particularly (and Africans generally) how they have (and urge them) to rise in unison and take proper independent control of their lives. Underlying the book's dominating Glorious-Revolutionary message is the fact that human rights are totally at the margin in Cameroon (the national case study), with the Chief Executive absolutely free to 'legislate' and 'legalize' oppression; all thanks to the folly of excluding the judiciary from the exercise of political power that was installed in Foumban where a so-called federation is claimed to have been born, fortified by the imprisonment of the judicial institution's independence and; therefore, Cameroon's own freedom. It is high time Cameroon and Cameroonians (Africa and Africans) utilize some of the strategies herein furnished to be freed from close to a century of colonial bondage under the confusing covers of 'independence' and of 'advanced democracy'. This long-distance governance is exposed in the chapters following using the *tumbu-tumbu* long-distance government theory (LDGT).

The first chapter traces the history and evolution of the folly of excluding the judiciary from the exercise of political power in Cameroon before critically studying the Chief Justice and the Supreme Court size, as well as the duties of Courts. Serious judicial reforms and principled emulation from countries like Canada, Belgium and Germany are suggested. Chapter 2 examines the role played in the judicial independence business by the methods of recruiting and training judges, magistrates, lawyers, teachers and other cadres of the state; showing that the entire recruitment and training scheme does not help in the matter of both personal and institutional integrity of teachers, judges, magistrates and lawyers; being solely aimed at maintaining and perpetuating judicial dependence and the flagrant administration of injustice. Better ways of recruitment and training are also proposed. Chapter 3 dutifully studies the marriage between federalism, the independent judiciary and justice administration; detailing out some constitutional fundamentals such as balance and supremacy of a community's Constitution; aspects that would easily exclude the *tumbu-tumbu* LDGT by guaranteeing both local governance and legality and rule of law. It is recommended that the all-time presence of an independent judiciary is one of the essential and unique institutions that help federalism achieve its mission and also make constitutionalism quite meaningful and understandable.

The fourth chapter advances some strategies on what ought to be done to have the generally recognized human rights organ (judiciary) freed for it to also liberate Cameroonians from the close to a century of bondage of the *tumbu-tumbu* Long-Distance Government (aka neo-colonialism) under the guise of 'independence' and 'advanced democracy'. While vehemently kicking against the encouragement of the dependency syndrome in Africa, the chapter demonstrates that Cameroonians can easily have the society of their dream even with their current 1996 Constitution: provided they are ready to firmly stand behind their judiciary, an independent institution which should then be able to competently turn said constitution into an enforceable Charter of Rights and Freedoms. The chapter (like the entire book) calls for vigorous and active citizenship from all, advising that the way to successfully defending human rights is collective and non-discriminatory. Since the protection of rights and freedoms is linked to an independent arbiter, securing judicial independence becomes both a necessity and a matter of the involvement of everyone in monitoring violations of not only their rights and freedoms, but also those of neighbours. There is a conclusion which is essentially that a whole lot of things would need to be done by Cameroonians in order to merit the "birds of the feather" description with countries like Canada. They must have to make the required changes and thereby be properly belonging to the Birds-of-the-Feather Club. In other words, Cameroonians must move the gear lever out of the reverse and into an appropriate forward gear; a thing Cameroonians (like Africans generally) can only successfully do if they eschew the schizophrenic drive to assimilate and instead formulate new ways of thinking and acting, new critical approaches to every social, political and juridical institutions, be they rooted in the east or in the west of Cameroon or Africa. It is my belief that this is not such a very difficult job to do: should the dedication and zeal to be free just be there.

CHAPTER 1

HUMAN RIGHTS AND JUDICIAL POLITICS IN CAMEROON: *IDEAS OF A COUNTRY THAT SHOULD LEAD AFRICA OUT OF THE DUNGEON*

As noted in the introduction, one notable state on the African continent that can be comfortably used interchangeably with it is no other than Cameroon which is also known as the microcosm of Africa. Federalism and rule of law issues are responsible for the human rights cataclysm in Cameroon – Africa's supposed legendary pathfinder. The chequered colonial history of Cameroon, according to Professor Oben Timothy Mbuagbo, saw the emergence of two distinct linguistic/cultural groups from the erstwhile German colony of Kamerun, born from the ashes of the Second World War; one, English-speaking (heretofore referred to as Anglophone Cameroon), the other French-speaking. These two independently administered regions formed, in 1961, a two-state federation (on the assumption of equality), then a United Republic in 1972 (Mbuagbo, 2002: 431). That unnecessary and frivolous *assumption* of equality from the Foumban arrangements, crisebacologists would think, is directly responsible for the worrisome human rights atmosphere in Cameroon; an air which thus

1

intensely compels a keen and critically balanced look at the country's judiciary, an institution that is almost always associated with human rights protection in most polities around the globe. Objective critique is what this book on human and cultural rights protection in beloved Cameroon and sweet Mother Africa is all about. These human and cultural rights are important ingredients of development and would appear to be excluded in the continent by the infamous tumbu-tumbu long-distance government theory (LDGT) that is nowhere so entrenched than in Cameroon. Readers could here liken the LDGT to Petit-Pays' popular *'fais-moi voyager sans décoler'* which is synonymous to comfortably sitting in an armchair in the *Champ d'Elysée* and 'governing' an unknown forest called Africa.

Since Cameroon is loudly boasting of being able and ready to export its own brand of democracy (see Fossungu, 2013b: xv & passim; 2018a: 147-51), it is only fair that the rest of the world also be aware of certain aspects of this exportable corruption or confusioncracy from Yaoundé. Because democracy necessarily involves an independent arbiter, prospective importers must want to know from the experts (see Tiruchelvam, 1987; Waltman, 1989; Goell, 1978; Beatty, 1994), for instance, how the country's judiciary has been fashioned to respond to the demands and problems of ethnic or cultural pluralism. At the trial level, for example, is there a single judge or a panel? Is the judge full-time? What about the bijuralism and bilingualism of the judge? Is there lay participation, either as jurors or quasi-judges? Are there panels at the appellate level or does the whole court sit on each case? Is there a chief judge, and if so, what is that person's influence? What is the role of counsel or advocate? In criminal cases, what is the role of the prosecuting authorities? What role does precedent play, formally or informally? What can be said of dissenting opinions? Are they kept private or made public? Do the judges' political perception colour their decision? What of the influence of those outside the court: legal academics, prominent counsel, the nation's chief legal officer? These are just a few of some of the issues that anyone who holds the doctrine of separation of powers and democracy dear to heart must want to know before making his or her decision whether or not to import 'advanced democracy'. This book also comes to aid such prospective importers make a decision that they would be comfortable with.

The book thus, attempts to expose why and how Cameroon's judiciary has not been able to live up to the tasks that are supposed to be its own; the most inhibiting of the responsible factors being the staggering absence of any iota of separation of powers. Cameroon is basically a single-branch (better still, *one-manish*, according to Fossungu [2013b]) governmental system: this being the proper way of explaining the abysmal human rights catastrophe Cameroonians are exposed to daily, being a direct result of the *tumbu-tumbu* long-distance governance. There is urgent need to arrest this disquieting situation and to restore constitutionalism and rule of law in Cameroon particularly and Africa in general. This contribution is thus heading to the legalization of human rights and justice administration: the exact reverse of what is currently in place, being the brainchild of the *tumbu-tumbu* LDGT which necessarily excludes federalism or decentralization – well known forms of local governance. There is a necessary marriage between federalism and the independent judiciary (see chapter 3 for more on this). Democracy, being pluralistic in nature, necessitates multiplicity of power centres and an independent arbiter. With the exception of the large number of *des démocrates ignorants* (silly democrats) that have infested Cameroon's legal profession and politics, such an arbiter, as all sensible democrats agree, is the judiciary that is now generally considered to be the "Third Branch of Government" (see Russell, 1987; Orban, 1991). Being the third branch of government means that the judiciary is of the government but not with it; which is simply another way of saying that it is useless in the absence of separation and multiplicity of power centres.

Laura-Stella Eposi Enonchong, a law professor at The University of Warwick, has examined Cameroon's approach to judicial accountability, focusing on its political accountability to the executive. Enonchong contends forcefully that the judiciary in Cameroon is excessively accountable to the executive, a position which has resulted to the absence of judicial independence; also highly suggesting that a constitutional reform is necessary to restructure the relationship between the executive and the judiciary and to reform the institution of judicial insulation in order to provide adequate balance between independence and accountability (Enonchong, 2012). It is mostly such essential reform that can make all the talk of human rights promotion and protection meaningful.

The ratification and domestication of international human rights instruments, according to Dr Avitus Agbor (2015), could be used as indices to determine a state's commitment to the promotion and protection of and respect for human rights. Within municipal legal systems, he contends, the judiciary is one of the stakeholders to fulfil these tasks. The doctor thinks that, as one of the organs of government, the judiciary can play a critical role in defining the content and evolution of both democracy and human rights. Even though Cameroon is a state party to numerous international human rights instruments, Dr Agbor`s critical analysis of Cameroon's institutional mechanisms reveals that there is a conspicuous incompatibility between these institutional mechanisms and the ideals of democracy and human rights. More specifically, according to his findings, the power of the judiciary, as stipulated in the Constitution, is very limited. His conclusion is that, this parochial mandate has had a heavy toll on first, the democratic evolution of the country; and secondly, on ensuring the promotion, protection of, and respect for, human rights (Agbor, 2015). All these experts and many more are heavily confirmed in this book, beginning from this chapter that has three main parts. The first examines Cameroon's purported exclusion of the judiciary from the exercise of state powers; the second studies the composition of the country's judicial institution; while the third examines its duties, including that of the impeachment of the Chief Executive.

THE HISTORY AND FALLOUTS OF THE CONFUSING SILLINESS OF JUDICIAL EXCLUSION IN POLITICS

An independent judiciary is the inevitable arbiter of the smooth functioning of any genuine or proper federation. Let those Cameroonians demanding for a return to the Foumban arrangements pay special attention to these crisebacological lectures. Both Dr HNA Enonchong and Dr Carlson Anyangwe have provided a general and elaborate discussion of Cameroon's federal 'Judicial Power and Organisation' (see Enonchong, 1967: 205-227; Anyangwe, 1987: chapters 8 & 9). Federalism is one of the three mechanisms that Professor John Mukum Mbaku of Weber State University in the United States of America (USA) proffers as feasible means for African states to protect human rights generally but especially minority rights (Mbaku, 2018). One of the other two mechanisms is rule of law which the UN Secretary-General Kofi Annan defined in 2004 to embody, inter alia, separation of powers (see Fombad, 2014: 417). This necessarily means that the judiciary is one of the three traditional branches of government. Because the "stability of modern constitutional government and the protection of the rights of the individuals under it are a seamless web" (Enonchong, 1967: xiii), to ignore the judiciary (as is clearly done by Cameroon's 1996

Constitution: see *Loi Nº 96-06 du 18 janvier 1996 portant révision de la Constitution du 02 juin 1972*(hereinafter 1996 Constitution)) in any polity claiming democracy and federalism "would be analogous to playing Hamlet without the Prince" (Enonchong, 1967: 88). The fatal consequences of this one-manish system in Cameroon are hard to entirely estimate; but a very worrisome trend has emerged from them that would now have indiscriminately transformed federalists, in the eyes of the majority of the English-speaking citizens, to the real enemies of Southern Cameroons, with outright independence (secession) being seen as the 'oracle of truth'. I have to first examine this federalism confusion before tackling the evolution of the silliness of playing Hamlet without its Prince.

THE FEDERALISM CONFUSION AS FALLING OUT OF SILLINESS?

For some frank answers to this query, one must indulge in constitutionally and legally 'Interrogating the Foumban Union' (Nkengasong, 2012; Mehier, 2014). It is interesting to reiterate that, according to Reverend Gerald Jumbam, for example, "[f]ederalists are cowards standing on the fence – neither cold nor hot. They have left substance to pursue shadows. The federalists do not know that it is their presence which is the triumph of the oppressor; it is the sight of them which is the Southern Cameroon's confusion and helplessness. Our oracle of truth is independence, and it looms high and has a reality, and its 'Truth can fight its battle. It has a reality in it, which shivers to pieces swords of earth'" (Jumban, 2017). Most English-speaking Cameroonians wouldn't want anything to do with federalism or decentralization anymore because "Federation No Longer Comments Itself to Us" with the independence narrative being seen as the 'imperative and necessity' if British Southern Cameroonsians have to be freed from colonial subjugation from French Cameroun (Anyangwe, 2017). As one independence advocate has gone on to lengthily elucidate:

> [w]e of the Southern Cameroons, if we act consistently with our history, we cannot be loyal subjects to the despicable and tyrannous Yaoundé government. Archbishop, you speak of Decentralization and you offer us it as the best gift you think fitting for the resolution of this crisis? We are determined to decline a gift so laden with spurious promises and deceitful propensities. And who can blame us for so doing? Who should be surprised that Yaoundé would still do to Buea what it did after the Foumban constitutional conference of 1961 – turn traitor to the very constitution that bound them together as brothers

with two equal strengths (and not that spurious decentralization you are talking about that wants to equate Buea with Garoua as if you do not know that Buea is the capital of a country and Garoua is a mere region of another country) or turn Cain against his brother Abel by killing everything we (Abel) had as culture, economy, jurisprudence, education, politics, military, etc (Jumban, 2017).

It is obvious that these are very hard and complicated issues. But this book unmistakably represents the centrepiece of 'My Idea of a Country That Leads Africa Out Of the Dungeon' and has been principally inspired by the Constitutional Politics of Belgium, of Canada, of Germany and of Switzerland. The contribution certainly may not be the ideal but I am still audaciously putting it forward, not being afraid to take a firm position; and being greatly fortified by the understanding that "None of these dilemmas has an easy or obvious answer. It is only by debating and challenging our own and others' perceptions and judgments that we, as lawyers and responsible citizens, can make sure that legislation and moral and ethical standards don't slip as a result of our lack of interest or concern" (Kentridge, 1995). Although the book advocates for both federalism and independence, it stands clear enough from both the Southern Cameroons 'federalists' and 'independentists'.

Let's get more of the nonsense that is growing fatter and fatter and blinding Cameroonians from seeing this country's colonial status from the tussle between these two Southern Cameroons camps which, one must stress, are clearly dueling in the dark (if readers also ask my straightforward view).

This contribution does not see eye-to-eye with the 'independentists' because (1) they are directing their freedom message to the wrong quarters or audience and against the inappropriate coloniser; and (2) they appear to be ready to have independence *granted* to them. Real freedom, as emphasized over and over in this book and elsewhere (see Fossungu, 2013b: chapter 2), is never granted, it is seized. It is thought that their independence messages (with the necessary substitutions) would make a lot of sense if directed to all Cameroonians – English-speaking and French-speaking alike – with the real coloniser (France) being unmistakably named in them. In the way they are put, their messages make little or no sense because the Southern Cameroons alone cannot obtain independence from a dependent colony (which they are mistakenly calling East Cameroun or LRC). Don't lawyers put it often in Latin the saying that you cannot give out what you do not have? The Republic of Cameroon (which now includes the Southern Cameroons, like it or not) is not independent and that is the singular reason the

English-speaking of this colony are being assimilated: since France just cannot tolerate the English-speaking and their inherited culture (in like manner as the British did to the French-speaking in Canada after vanquishing the French on the Plains of Abraham) within its colony. The penetrating discussion of Cameroon's 'Poorest-ugliest French Bijuralism Horse' (Fossungu, 2018a) further explains the point.

The Independence Question must have to be reframed accordingly so that Cameroonians (from North to South and from East to West) can rise in unison as a people and nation and snatch their independence from the colonial yoke of that European country called France. That is the independence objective of this book and more strategies for accomplishing the mission are scattered in its chapters. The manner most of the English-speaking Cameroonians are and have been going about it only furthers the Divide-and-Rule technique to the pleasure of the coloniser, France; and not East Cameroun, as the Southern Cameroons independence advocates would appear to think. Sensitization of the entire Cameroonian population (*à la Upéciste*) regarding the need to free their country from colonial bondage is the essential education and message that should now be spreading to all the corners of the neo-colony.

Therefore, the advocacy of this book is for the federalism that many nations have adopted in order to be free from or independent of foreign domination and that genre of federalism is fully in line with what I have already prescribed in 2013 in my *Democracy and Human Rights in Africa* (Fossungu, 2013b). Such proper federalism will go a long way to strangle the substance out of the tumbu-tumbu LDGT alias the *Developer Theory*. The developer theory, "very briefly stated, prevents or subverts the institution of Western democracy in the developing states because it would be tantamount to breaking the back of the developer: And, consequently, an end to their nicely camouflaged job of developing the 'developed' or First World" (Fossungu, 1998c, original emphasis; also see Mhango, 2018). This is where the book differs stiffly with the Southern Cameroons federalists' position since (1) they not only are very unconvincing but also want a return to a federation that never existed; and (2) they are mostly opportunistic and still believe in the same one-manish way of the President of the Republic (POR) and his barons authorizing that federation. Readers can get their silliness here from Dr Munzu's argument that provoked Dr Anyangwe's. "Dr. Anyangwe's argument came in the framework of a narrative led by Dr. Simon Munzu and others suggesting that Southern Cameroonians have no recourse to independence through the United Nations because no such provisions exist in the treaties merging the Southern Cameroons with LRC [La République du Cameroun]. Munzu submits that federation is the utmost Southern Cameroons can ask for from La République du Cameroun" (Anyangwe, 2017). It is just as Cameroonians also waited for the POR to authorize multipartism in 1990; and what do we have today as that authorized multipartism? More concentration of powers in the POR's hands than even before the said multipartism! Instituting the federal system or democracy in this country is not *something* to be permitted by an individual. It has to be a collective venture and this country has more than enough experts on the issues of independence and democratic governance, to name just these here. Let them all come out of their hiding places and fix Cameroon for Cameroonians. That is a challenge.

I would thus be leaning toward and preaching the national federalist cause (as opposed to the limited Southern Cameroons opportunists being called 'federalists') since the advocates of this national (and continental) brand appear to be more convincing and embracing a larger picture perspective that I think is what Africa really needs to be able to make a difference on the world stage. I have thus strenuously argued against the secessionists when, talking of successfully managing a country, for instance, I sent the following message in 1998 to the advocates of secession in Cameroon:

Rather than scrutinize and fight against some of these anomalies, this Second Home country's Anglophones, in particular, would only be fighting themselves. And then some of these same adventurers (after having failed to gain the First Home ticket for which they fight themselves) would come up to further play on the confused and rudderless citizens' fear and uncertainty with their idea of secession (another Second Home?). Next time you see them, tell them this: We belong here and simply talking of secession rather than correcting the flaws of this society of ours is, to say the least, escapist. We must cease running away from our responsibilities to our children.

If Anglophones cannot stand up together against this common threat to their collective survival, just how (we must be constantly asking the secessionists) can they even be able to manage a country – assuming they succeed in seceding? If you then ask my view, here is it: We must fight for equality, justice, and freedom in Cameroon. Note also that in 1972 (the year when their secession talk would have been musically sweetest to both the ear and mind) they rather UNITED us then (Fossungu, 1998a).

In 2013 I also made it clear that Foumban-based postulations "like this one [from the 'Return-to-Foumban' federalists] forcefully portray to me that a lot of Cameroonians have not yet learnt anything from the past fifty-three or so years, most probably because of the confusioncracy. That they are still to come to grips with the fact that the personification of public debates in this country and the associated alarming human rights questions are intimately rooted in the events that took place before and during the Foumban Conference" (Fossungu, 2013b: xii). Foumban is too often erroneously equated with Philadelphia in the USA, especially by the English-speaking Cameroonians despite overwhelming evidence to the contrary. In my 2013 book that is described by Dr Piet Konings of the African Studies Centre in Leiden as "a provocative but masterful study of federalism in Africa... [that] provides us with many constructive building-stones for the creation of truly federal states in Africa" (ibid: back cover, omission added), I argued compellingly that "[m]y firm belief is that Cameroon should be uniting Africa rather than further splitting the continent into incapable mini-states vis-à-vis the changing world stage" (ibid: x). I went on to elaborately demonstrate in the book that there has never been any federation created in Cameroon: meaning that this state governing modality has to be attempted now. I concluded that "[t]he secession-from-federalism theses in this country have no firm bases except those of calculatingly blinding Cameroonians of the need to look to countries like Canada, Belgium, Germany, and Switzerland for ground rules to the type of society they are now seeking" (ibid: xii).

It is thought that it is only in this 'confusioncracy' context that the generalized charges against federalists and other postulations based on the Foumban Union (like Reverend Jumbam's) could be better grasped. Some analysts see in them what they brand as conflicting narratives from 'political opportunists' who are merely 'Exploiting Anglophone Identity in State Deconstruction' (see Mbuagbo, 2002; Takougang, 2003). Thus, agreeing that the 'feeling' of communal disadvantage is widespread within the Cameroon Anglophone community, Dr Dickson Eyoh of the University of Buea (UNIBU) contends that Anglophone elites offer contending explanations for the roots of, and visions for, the best political solution to the so-called Anglophone problem. The UNIBU professor has therefore focused his discussion on the construction and use of social memories of the post-colonial trajectory to evaluate rival explanations of the origins and proposals for the redress of the Anglophone problem (Eyoh, 1998). These exploitative, opportunistic and conflicting narratives would thus also forcefully make the case for the necessity of an independent judiciary. This is an institution that is better placed to authoritatively say whose view of the Cameroon state reflects the constitution that should normally be under that institution`s jurisdiction to interpret and give life to. Thus, this contribution would tend to concord with the idea that "Africans should be able to comprehend that, when it is what it is or ought to be, federalism cannot be detached from effective multiparty politics or constitutional democracy; that it must guarantee judicial independence, fundamental human rights, and local values and minority concerns" (Fossungu, 2013b: x).

All those things are inconceivable in the stark absence of separation of powers. According to Professor John Mukum Mbaku (2014), countries incorporate the principle of the separation of powers, including judicial independence, into their constitutions in an effort to meet several goals, the most important of which is to minimise government-induced tyranny. Specifically, countries that make this principle part of their constitutional practice intend to limit public servants by national laws and institutions, enhance government accountability, minimise opportunistic behaviours by civil servants and politicians, provide for checks and balances, and generally improve government efficiency. Cameroon, part of which was colonised by France, according to the professor, has a constitution that is modelled closely on the French Constitution of 4 October 1958. As a consequence, the country has adopted France's hybrid system of the separation of powers. Using French constitutional practice as a model, Mbaku has gone on to examine constitutional developments in Cameroon to determine why the country's governing process, which is based on the Constitution of the Fifth Republic, has failed to guarantee constitutional justice (Mbaku, 2014).

The shortest explanation could be related, for instance, to the role of French courts (see Radamaker, 1987) and to effective multipartsm and the fact that national interest is prioritized in France (see Fossungu, 2013a: chapter 3). Very unlike what obtains in France, there is simply no room for compromise in a completely one-manish system such as Cameroon's; a system of government properly defined by the French-speaking of this country as a 'debateless democracy' ('*une démocratie sans débat, donc sans compromise*' (Sibafo, 1996). That properly elucidates why, rather than debating and compromising, the case, is as Jubah (2017) put's it in one of his speeches:

[d]arkness [that] has descended on the British Cameroons in the killings, imprisonments, abductions, rapes, graves of mass burials and maim. Bamenda/Buea is facing viral alteration of psychic conditioning. In this state of affairs, silence is criminal. The sense of urgency has lagged so much that a month ago I lost my anger on a letter to a compatriot invading media space with the banner, screaming: Homecoming or Home-going – the Southern Cameroons! It is a wakeup call no more on failed internal religious and political bodies, but on Britain and International Human rights institutions and activists, not to delay, because what happened in Rwanda is at our doors. AU and UNO look up and act! UK look up and speak! The urgency of speaking for despoiled peoples is so felt that I don't really care if this anger breaks the bounds of office. How could it be when a priest is first and foremost a citizen? He owes his community a contribution to its wellbeing for his upbringing. He serves God and recognizes that the cry of the powerless and the voice of the voiceless is [are?] the cry and the voice of God (Jumban, 2017).

HUMAN RIGHTS CATASTROPHE FROM PLAYING HAMLET WITHOUT THE PRINCE?

This second section traces the history of judicial marginalization or exclusion. Playing Hamlet without the Prince is exactly what the Foumban Enterprise or Federal Constitution (see, *Loi № 61-24 du 1er septembre 1961 portant révision constitutionnelle et tendant à adapter la constitution actuelle aux nécessités du Cameroun réunifié* (hereinafter Federal Constitution)) has meant. This document is the taproot of all the confusion in Cameroon to date; properly explaining why in Cameroon it is the presidentially-appointed President (Speaker, to Americans, Australians, and Canadians) of the National Assembly that must administer the Oath of Office to the Chief Executive called President of the Republic (POR). Hence, according to Article 7 (2) of the 1996 Constitution, "he [the POR] shall take the Oath of Office before the Cameroonian people, in the presence of the members of Parliament, the Constitutional Council and the Supreme Court meeting in solemn session... [being] sworn in by the President of the National Assembly." It should be noted that this provision finds its roots in the so-called federal epoch. The Federal Constitution in Article 10 merely talked of the president taking "the oath in the form prescribed by Federal law." Nowhere in that federal document, especially in its Title VI which deals with 'The

Judicial Authority' (Articles 32-35) was anything said that it is one of the duties of the Federal Court of Justice (FCJ – Articles 33-34) or even the Federal Council of Magistracy (FCM – Article 32) to administer such oaths. Similarly, the 1972 Constitution of the United Republic of Cameroon (see 2 June 1972 Constitution of the United Republic of Cameroon) simply stated in Article 7(3) that the POR "shall take the oath in the manner laid down by the law", a position that is not altered in Article 7(2) of the 1984 Constitution (see *Loi Nº 84-1 du 4 février 1984* (hereinafter 1984 Constitution)). One can thus see that it is only the 1996 Constitution that has very boldly made room in the document itself as to how that oath is to be taken and who is to administer it. All this, according to the critics like Justice Nyo'Wakai of the Cameroon Supreme Court (CSC), is plainly "to say [in effect to the ignored judiciary], never mind, we shall run the affairs our own way, i.e., the political way" (Nyo'Wakai, 1991: 18). Anyangwe (1987: 142) also says the same thing.

Other parts of this country's confusing Constitutions would seem to confirm the charge of these critics. Not only is the 1996 Constitution to replace the Supreme Court with a so-called Constitutional Council in Article 67(4): "The Supreme Court shall perform the duties of the Constitutional Council until the latter is set up." In addition, according to Article 4 of the same

Constitution, "[s]tate power shall be exercised [only] by: The President of the Republic [and] Parliament." Yet the Cameroon judiciary, for the very first time, has been uplifted from its former status of 'judicial authority' to 'judicial power' in the 1996 Constitution's Part V (Articles 37-42). It is stated, for instance, in Article 37(2) how *"Judicial Power* shall be exercised by the Supreme Court, Courts of Appeal and Tribunals. The *Judicial Power* shall be independent of the executive and legislative powers. Magistrates of the bench shall, in the discharge of their duties, be governed only by the law and their conscience" (emphasis is supplied). It must be reiterated that the 1996 Article 4 in question has always been there. It has an interesting genesis and curious life span. Originating as Article 4 of the 1961 Federal Constitution, it then retained itself in the 1972 Constitution as its Article 4; staying on and refusing to change twelve years later in Article 4 of the 1984 Constitution, before maturing and graduating (with the replacement-distinction of Article 67(4) and the confusioncracy of Article 37(2)) into its current status.

It is also of interest that the 'intellectuals in politics' decided during the surprisingly short One-Hour-35-Minute Foumban Constitutional Talks that the President of the Federal Republic should 'guard' judicial independence in the Federal Constitution's Article 32, 2nd paragraph. In 1972 when that 'Federal' Article metamorphosed into Article 31 of the Unitary Constitution, 'guards' was substituted with 'ensures'; which has itself also been replaced by the present 1996 'guarantees' in Article 37(3). This 'guaranteeing' of judicial independence incomprehensibly comes only at the same time as the institution (which has now been uplifted to the status of 'judicial power'): (1) has been very cruelly regulated (see Fossungu, 2013a: 136-37), and (2) is expressly NOT to exercise 'state powers' of any sort. Now, is 'judicial power' not embedded in 'State powers'? The kind of tautology or paradox here is obviously open to the logician's objection; all this being reminiscent of the country's *Advanced* [killing of] *Democracy*.

No one's words decipher that the advanced killing of democracy is what is involved in Cameroon better than those of Herbert George Nicholas, of Frank M. Stark and of Peter Ateh-Afac Fossungu. In finding some kind of fault with the United Nations and its preamble, Nicholas points out that, as a title for a permanent organization, 'United Nations' "is no doubt open to the logician's objection that it assumes as an historic fact a unity which the organization has been created to promote" (Nicholas, 1963: 2). There is either a tautology or a contradiction, Nicholas continues, about the preamble to the UN

Charter, with its phrase, "We, the peoples of the United Nations determined... to unite our strength." If so, he concludes, "it merely enshrines a paradox common to many forms of human endeavour; that some concept of the end must inhere in the beginning – alternatively that even a beginning cannot be made until there has been some progress towards that end" (ibid). Also analyzing the shadow and reality of the Cameroon federation, Stark (1976: 424-37) discusses 'The End Before the Beginning, while Fossungu (2015b: 108), in discussing the fabricated lies relating to Africa, declares that "I would have liked you to first eat before using the toilet. But sometimes the end becomes a better beginning, justifying why I want us to kick-start *Lielisticalism* with *shitting* business" (original emphasis) That shitting business here concerns the demise of the judiciary in Cameroon that was initiated in Foumban which is, of course, that end. This theory is sufficiently corroborated by the fact that the Foumban Constitution is the only among Cameroon's plethora of constitutions that does not have a preamble, nor make the empty and misleading upside-down 'Pride in Diversity' declaration. Foumban, as this book further demonstrates, entirely centralized and concentrated powers in all spheres to an extent that talking of an 'Anglophone Cameroon' is purely confusing, a confusion dubbed by some critics as synonymous to 'Distinguishing

God from God' (Fossungu, 2018a: 130-51), which "is just a neat and tidy philosophical way of saying 'it is a needlessly senseless distinction'" (ibid: 130). This seems to be the exact reverse of the Canadian experience where confederation kind of liberated Quebec from the United Province of Canada (that was made up of current Ontario and Quebec).

The upside-down situation in Cameroon is largely tied to the absence of an independent judicial institution, whose foolish exclusion from exercise of 'state powers' finds its roots in the so-called Federal Constitution. It is just so silly trying to keep the judiciary out of the business as Professor G.A.G. Griffith theorizes firmly in 1977 in his *The Politics of the Judiciary* that democracy necessarily requires "that some [independent] group of persons acts as an arbiter not only between individuals but also between Governmental power and the individual" (Anyangwe, 1989: 22). Cameroon's Federal Constitution which gave birth to the silliness, like all the others indiscriminately and confusioncratically marching behind it, is very far from being supreme. On the contrary, a country's Constitution really ought to be a supreme and preponderant law that is respected by everyone, big or small, high or low, government official or ordinary citizen. An elaborate study of those attributes of the Constitution is offered in chapter 3. This chapter will next examine the status and duties of the courts, an exercise that would further expose the nonsensical tumbu-tumbu LDGT approach in Cameroon, a scheme that is geared only toward perpetuating inhuman rights and injustice legalization and thus also guaranteeing the *developer theory*. That is to announce that we are about entering into the second and third parts devoted to the *Judicial Composition and Role in Bicultural Societies*, under which one would principally examine (1) the Chief Justice and Supreme Court size, and (2) the constitutional and other duties of Courts, especially highlighted by the impossibility of impeaching the nation's president-chief justice-sole-legislator.

THE CHIEF JUSTICE AND THE SIZE OF THE CAMEROON SUPREME COURT

The status, powers and role of any country's Apex Court or Supreme Court are very intimately tied to those of the head of the institution – the Chief Justice. Chief Justices around the world have greatly impacted on the development of their respective countries. Chief Justice John Marshall of the United States of America very easily comes to mind here. Thus, as a criminal-law-and-society expert has powerfully indicated:

[w]hen Chief Justice Marshall in 1803 read the doctrine of judicial supremacy into the 4,373 words of the Constitution of the United States he made it a living document and, at the same time, he made the Court the guardian of personal liberties. From that time to the present time, that Constitution has been construed to mean that law is not only to govern relations between man and man; it is to govern as well the government itself. Law applies to all persons, public or private, high or low, even to the President (Day, 1964: 34).

The attributes of the chief justice would thus be highlighted before the discussion of the size of the Supreme Court. We can also illustrate the point with the case of Chief Justice (or Lord Chancellor) Coke of England. Lord Hailsham of Marylebone (1989) has offered an elaborate analysis of the Lord Chancellor's status, powers and role in Britain. As Lord Denning and others recount, Chief Justice Coke boldly asserted the independence of the judges and, time after time, he clashed with the King over it. The king at one point even sought to interfere with a decision of the judges on a case by telling them not to proceed with it until they had consulted him. Coke resolutely refused, saying that to obey His Majesty's command to stay proceedings would be a delay of justice, contrary to the law, and to the oaths of the judges. In the trial of the Seven Bishops in 1688 for publicly asserting that the King had no power to dispense with the laws of England (as some subservient judges had gone on at one point to hold), the jury acquitted them; thus, inferentially holding that the King had no such dispensing power (see Denning, 1955: 10-11; Loewenstein, 1967: 167; Pasquet, 1968; Gwyn, 1965: 6). Is that not how the intellectuals of Cameroon should go about it? Even in the Canadian Supreme Court's passivism days, there were powerful dissenting judgments coming from great jurists like Chief Justice Bora Laskin, who did not hesitate to indicate where the law was contrary to contemporary social values, and thereby shamed legislators into changing it (Mallory, 1984: vii). Canadian Institute for the Administration of Justice (1981) furnishes an elaborate study of the chief justice's status, powers and role in Canada.

On the other hand, due to a number of reasons that all hinge on the absence of separation of powers, there have been no innovative judgments in Cameroon, even when the Cameroon Supreme Court has had several volcanic occasions on which to shame the legislators. A typical example is the *Affaire SGTE* case (C.J.F. Arrêt Nº4, 28 Octobre 1970, (1960-1970) 1 *Recueil Mbonyoum*). A further incisive discussion of this case has been furnished by Fossungu (2013b: 146-50). This unfortunate case decided that (1) the preamble has no constitutional importance and is not part and parcel of the Constitution, and (2) no one else but the POR can challenge the constitutionality or otherwise of any law or constitution as per the constitution itself. The constitutional provision that the court was here using to sustain the second arm of its decision is Article 10 of Cameroon's 1972 Constitution, a provision which finds its roots in the 1961 Federal Constitution's Article 14 by which "The President of the Federal Republic shall refer to the Federal Court of Justice, constituted as provided in Article 34, any Federal law which he considers to be contrary to the present Constitution or any law of either of the Federated States which he regards as having been adopted in violation of the provisions of the Constitution or a federal law." The next part of this chapter talks a little more on the issue when the duties of courts are examined. The absence of separation of the judiciary from the executive head is also reinforced by (1) the Cameroon Penal Code (being both *Loi Nº 65-LF-24 du 12 novembre 1965 & Loi Nº 67- LF-1 du 12 juin 1967*(hereinafter CPC)) – as discussed in chapter 2, and (2) the government-imposed professional *solidarity* which must be seen to exist among Supreme Court judges so that none of them can decide a case in his or her unique way.

PROMOTING COURT SOLIDARITY OR REINFORCING JUDICIAL DEPENDENCE?

This other strategy of incapacitating judicial adventurism is attained through (1) the official insistence on an *esprit de corps* or court solidarity, and (2) the principle of deciding cases by panel, without dissenting judgments: reinforced by the *"secret de la délibération"* rule, which means that every judgment is the product of the collective examination by all the judges concerned (see Anyangwe ,1989: 31-32; & *Loi Nº 75/16 du 08 décembre 1975 fixant la procédure et le fonctionnement de la Cour suprême*). As one of the Apex Court's own justices and other critics have put it, the entire procedure of the CSC and the manner of regulating it unambiguously constitute a clog on justice. Heightening this justice-clogging process is the CSC *renvoi* which, in theory, "can go on ad infinitum... [and] explains why cases take up to ten years in the Supreme Court before a decision is handed down. Our Supreme Court, as I see it, is ineffective because ... the [entire] procedure is a clog on justice. The crowds one sees around the Supreme Court are there to personally follow up their case files" (Nyo'Wakai, 1991: 18; also see Ewang, 1995). Where is the institutionalized guarantee of justice then, as claimed by some 'intellectuals in politics'? The question is especially pertinent because this Court cannot act unless moved by the POR (see Duties of Courts below). All this should not have been possible if there was a federation proper created in 1961 in Foumban, since a federal Constitution must necessarily be balanced and supreme (see Wheare, 1963). This confusing justice-clogging state of affairs in Cameroon has even been brought about by the same acclaimed Foumban Federal Constitution. There is not much else which can be said about the chief justice (or president of the CSC) that is divorced from the composition and functioning of the institution she or he supposedly heads.

THE NUMERICAL MYSTERY OF NUMBERS AND HEADS

The composition and functioning of the highest court of the land are matters of enhanced importance to cultural groups in most multicultural polities. It is worth noting that *most* is used because *all* would be clearly out of place since Cameroon forcefully objects. These aspects are particularly significant in polities with more than one official language. That is, multilingual and/or bicultural societies. For instance, Evan Joel Shapiro informs us that linguistic parity is scrupulously respected in the composition and functioning of the Belgian Apex Court. Six of its twelve members are French-speaking while the remaining six are Dutch-speaking. At least one member must be German-speaking [meaning it is instead a 13-member court?]. The Belgian Office of Chief Justice alternates each year between the presidents of these two groups, who are elected by their respective members. The Court usually sits in panels composed of the two Presidents and five other members, who hand down per curium decisions with no dissenting opinions (Shapiro, 1995: 67). Although there is no mandatory alternation of its head between the two cultural groups in Canada, three of the nine Supreme Court justices must be from Quebec (see Russell, 1969). What is the position like in Cameroon? It is a total mystery! Another funny story!

THE HEAD SECOND-FIDDLE JEOPARDY GAME

Cameroon will very much laugh at the Belgians for talking and attempting parity with the minority; and at Canadians for apportioning a specific ratio. Let us leave aside its composition for a while and first talk about the presidency (that is, the rough equivalent of Chief Justice-ship) of the CSC. Although there is a president of the CSC, that position proper must be forgotten because of the 1996 Constitution and its forerunners. It is the "President of the Republic [of Cameroon who still] shall guarantee the independence of judicial power.... appoint[ing] members of the bench and of the legal department" in Article 37(3) of the 1996 Constitution. As noted above, this provision originated as Article 32 of the 1961 Federal Constitution (with the president 'guarding' that independence) and then became Article 31 of the 1972 Constitution (with the president 'ensuring' it). It then graduated as Article 31 of the 1984 Constitution, then to the present context. The question becomes that of where the separation of powers is. And why does Cameroon still have a president of the CSC except for the purpose of confusion while realizing more concentration of powers?

While Charles Manga Fombad, a law professor at the University of Pretoria (South Africa), describes it very tersely as "nothing more than tokenistic and symbolic constitutionalism" (Fombad, 2014: 412) which explains the staggering 'Failed Democratic Transition in Cameroon' (Dicklitch, 2002), Professor Ericka Albaugh has an intriguing lengthy answer that goes a long way to reinforcing the political naivety and opportunism exposition above. According to Albaugh, Cameroon's President Paul Biya has weathered the transition from a single-party to a multi-party system, dramatically strengthening his control over the political apparatus in recent years. While many have noted the tendency of Africa's new 'democrats' to consolidate their authority by removing various constitutional restraints on their power, **Albaugh** argues skilfully that Biya has adapted more subtly to the various opportunities provided by open political competition and international discourse on minority rights. Beyond the sadly predictable fraud in electoral counting, **Albaugh** affirms, Biya has manipulated electoral boundaries to his party's advantage, while at the same time prohibiting voting access to citizens who would likely vote for the opposition. In addition, the political science professor concludes, Biya has acceded to constitutional changes to recognize minorities in compliance with international and domestic pressures, which is in reality yet another useful tool to marginalize the opposition (Albaugh, 2012). One of those helpful tools is the fact that **the separate post of Chief Justice as such does not therefore exist in Cameroon. Importers of Advanced Democracy beware!**

But the reader must from time to time, in the course of reading about Cameroon injustice administration, come across a certain Chief Justice E.M.L Endeley. How come? An explanation of this curious phenomenon must take us further deep down into the 'Second Fiddle Syndrome and Irrational Pride' (Fossungu, 2018a: 139-44) of the English-speaking of this country. Any such title still being borne today in Cameroon results from

Anglophone constitutional, political and judicial subordination instituted by a federal law (see *Ordinance N° 61/OF/6 of 6 October 1961*, as amended by *Decree N° 64/DF/218 of 19 June 1964* and *Law N° 69/LF1 of 14 June 1969*), which (like the 1961 Federal Constitution did to their Prime Minister in Article 52) also made the 'president' of East Cameroon's Supreme Court the automatic permanent president of the Federal Court of Justice (FCJ) – predecessor of current CSC – with the Chief Justice of West Cameroon being only one of the five substantive judges of this FCJ (which had four alternate judges). Dr Carlson Anyangwe provides much more details of this curious arrangement (see Anyangwe, 1987: 139 et seq). Asked to compare the position in West Cameroon before and after the 1972 transformation, an Anglophone judge of the CSC stated in regard of the 'Chief Justice' as follows in a 1991 Special Political Issue of *Le Messager*:

> ... For example, the head of the judiciary [in West Cameroon] was well honoured and lodged in a palace. One of the shocks I had when I got to Yaoundé for the first time was the fact that the President of the Supreme Court in the person of Mr. NGUINI was living in a tumble-over house while boys who had just graduated from ENAM and appointed Ministers were living in palaces. Mr. NGUINI endured his ordeal until

a few years to his retirement. Even then the supposed new lodge allocated to him had been vacated by a junior Minister for being sub-standard. Nobody bothered about the personal security of President NGUINI whereas in West Cameroon, all High Court Judges were provided with Orderlies and State Counsels going on assizes had a Police Constable assigned to them. Also the protocol position of the Magistrates or Judges left no doubt in anyone's mind that they represented a power (Nyo'Wakai, 1991: 18).

THE POR'S SECRET OF DOUBLING THE UNCONVENTIONAL KNOWLEDGE AND EXPERIENCE

What a contrast! Yet, all that is regarded as very normal by the country's myriad of 'intellectuals in politics'. Where actually is the place of rationality, justice, equality, 'brilliance', 'the achievement of future self-government', 'independence' and 'fuller freedom of Anglophone Cameroonians' (as some Anglophone intellectuals do claim to be the gains of Foumban)? Don't we often say: 'To be forewarned is to be forearmed'? Shouldn't the Belgian Court formula now be emulated in Cameroon? Or even the Canadian? But how can these formulae even be adopted until we know the size of the

Court in question? Leaving the strangely unasked question of Anglophone representation in it, the composition of the CSC is not only unusual but seemingly beyond comprehension, even to the judges themselves (or maybe they know this?). The CSC's maximum number, which has never been indicated in any of the numerous constitutions, will forever remain a mystery to everyone else but the POR-Chief Justice. The CSC is composed of "the Chief Justice of the Court, Bench Presidents, Substantive and Alternate Puisne Judges, the Attorney General of the Court, an Advocate General, Deputies to the Procureur General, a Registrar-in-Chief and Registrars" (Anyangwe, 1987: 168). What is the actual number then?

The 1996 Constitution does not help us in the matter at all. It merely states in Article 38(1) that the Supreme Court is "the highest court of the State in legal and administrative matters as well as in the appraisal of accounts" and in Article 38(2) that it "shall comprise: - a judicial bench; - an administrative bench; - an audit bench." The duties of these three benches are outlined in Articles 39, 40, and 41, respectively. Neither is the situation ameliorated by certain constitutional duties that the CSC is to perform. On certain matters, that is to say, where this "Supreme Court is called upon to give an opinion in the cases contemplated by Articles 7, 10 and 27, its numbers shall be *doubled* by the addition of personalities nominated for one year by the *President of the Republic in view of their special knowledge or experience"* (1972 Constitution, Article 33: emphasis added). The Federal Constitution's Article 34 is to the same effect. The 1996 Constitution's Constitutional Council (Articles 46-52) has replaced this strategy which is clearly Biya's enterprising means of eternalizing himself in power, a modus that both Fombad (1998) and Fossungu (1998b) have not only brilliantly exposed but also stiffly and largely questioned.

There are several issues raised concerning the contemplated matters of the enumerated constitutional Articles and some of them are discussed in the next sections. For now, we simply want to know the actual number of the CSC that is to be doubled. In addition, how special are the knowledge and experience to be to satisfy the requirement? All these are solely at the POR's exclusive discretion. What about the clear definitions of all relationships among members which Biya (1986: 37) says are the hallmark of Cameroonian *advanced democracy*? Is the democracy really defined by confusion or by clarity? One would want to think that all this is simply another excellent means for incapacitating the CSC so that it can never, never be able to stand up against executive lawlessness that is passing under the name of order and tranquillity in this country. The duties reserved for courts in Cameroon will also buttress this never-never theory.

ADVANCED REMOTE CONTROLLITICS: DUTIES OF COURTS AND THE POSSIBLY IMPOSSIBLE IMPEACHMENT

Apart from their expressly stated constitutional duties enumerated in Articles 7, 10 and 27 of the 1972 Constitution, courts in Cameroon, by the Cameroon President's definition of the role of Courts, are to (1) render justice impartially; (2) guarantee rights and freedoms of the individual citizens and state organs; (3) settle disputes and (4) prevent crime by identifying offenders so that they may be punished. That is all coming from President Amadou Ahidjo's speech during the Supreme Court's 'Rentrée solennelle' in 1977, as quoted in Anyangwe (1989: 22 & 23). Recalling Section 126 of the Cameroon Penal Code (to be noted in chapter 2 below) that prohibits judicial officials from issuing any order whatsoever to executive officials, one cannot help questioning just how all this ties in with the Court's first three duties here. One has to further remember and note always that the POR of Cameroon is the only one to "define the policy of the nation" (1996 Constitution, Articles 5(2) & 11): with this policy definition normally surpassing any in the un-laid-down constitutions. What do lawyers particularly say and do about the fourth strange role of courts and other constitutional abnormalities in Cameroon?

The best way to continue digging into the matter is to find out the answer to this central question: What is the legal culture that is reserved for Cameroon? The issue is very important because a country's legal culture is a keen reflection of the attitudes or perspectives of its lawyers. In 1969 J.H. Merryman defined legal culture in his *The Civil Law Tradition* as a set of deeply rooted, historically conditioned attitudes about the nature of law, about the role of law in a society and the polity, about the proper organization and operation of the legal system, and about the way law is or should be made, applied, perfected, and taught (cited in Waltman, 1989: 3). Mallory (1984: 4-5); and Russell (1987: 35-39) provide the general details of Canadian legal culture. Generally speaking, a perspective is a way of looking at things; and will resolve for its proponents the question of what should be studied, how it should be studied, and how the study can contribute to reforming society and the basic knowledge in the field in which the perspective is held (Rubington and Weinberg, 1981: 9, 12 & 10). So, how are lawyers in Cameroon viewing these matters in question?

Professor Carlson Anyangwe who rightly thinks the fourth role of the courts "is a slight shift from the traditional role often assigned to judges" nevertheless quickly turns around (like Professors Pougoué and Kamto – see Fossungu (2013b: chapter 3)) to maintain that "this 'new' role does not mean that the judiciary would have to usurp the functions of the police. It is simply another way of saying the judiciary should be as much concerned as the executive with the preservation of law and order in society" (Anyangwe, 1989: 22). Fossungu has, on his part, more extensively critiqued this particular escapist stance in the academia; concluding that the express statement of that policing role "amounts, in my view, simply to this. The intention is to put the *magistrat* or judge on his or her guard by making it very pellucid to him or her that 'whenever the government accuses or even merely suspects anyone you must convict him or her without much ado'. The interpretation I have proffered here is sufficiently corroborated by a number of factors, four of which can be briefly outlined" (Fossungu, 1999a: 10). And the politico-socio-legal critic actually went on to persuasively do so.

The factors that Fossungu advances are so important for understanding this whole question of inhuman rights and illegality in Cameroon that laying them out here is thought to be necessary. The first, as

Fossungu noted, might come from President Julius Nyerere of Tanzania who could not help stating (concerning courts which acquit persons accused by the government) that "we have a problem on what to do with these people. However, we have not yet decided on the course of action. I ask the magistrates to forgive us if we hesitate to take culprits to courts of law. At times racketeers have been taken to courts where they either receive light sentences or have been set free..." (citing from Wambali and Peter, 1987: 139-40). The second factor, according to Fossungu, relates to the fact that security officers (of the police and gendarmerie) spy on judges (citing Anyangwe, 1989: 47-48), while the third is the fact that, in this country called Cameroon, one's prosecutor of the morning easily (and legally too) becomes one's judge in the afternoon, and by evening he or she is the administrator of one's prison (citing Anyangwe, 1989: 3 & 42; and Etahoben, 1990). And it is an open secret, Fossungu's argument goes on, that prosecutorial discretion in this country is far too wide and often abused (citing Anyangwe, 1989: xii-xiii & chapters 4 & 5; & Ewang, 1997: 41-44) by a department that is clearly not used to democratic methods (citing "The Prosecution Is Not Used to Democratic Methods" *Cameroon Post* of 20-25 May 1990, p. 6). The fourth reason given by the critic relates to the penal-coding of separation of powers which is discussed in chapter 2 below, together with Dr Anyangwe`s own interpretation of the judges' role from it. To Fossungu, "[o]ne may even add, as a fifth factor, the same *Code Pénal's Outrage au Président de la République*: regarding which *La vérité du fait diffamatoire ne peut en aucun cas être rapportée*" (citing CPC, Section 153(1) & (3), respectively). With a lot of soul-searching questions raised, Fossungu's sane conclusion is that the "whole arrangement, to shorten a long tragic story, makes first class mockery of justice administration. Do Cameroonians not deserve much more than this caricature of justice? How could the lawyers of this country then be demanding justice and liberty from a judiciary whose independence they do not care about?" (Fossungu, 1999a: 10). What support is the court in Cameroon going to obtain from the divisive legal profession and escapist academia in resolving the awkward constitutional and other issues? How can these courts be able to perform the roles traditionally assigned to them in a country whose constitutions lack balance and supremacy? Let's attempt a few answers using (1) advanced remote *controllitics*, and (2) impeaching the impeacher.

ADVANCED REMOTE CONTROLLITICS MEANS IMPOSSIBLE NEVER REALLY CAMEROONIAN?

The CSC can only entertain complaints against administrative acts where one is claiming damages or on grounds of ultra vires; and in connection with disputes regarding Articles 7, 10, and 27 of the Constitution, which the law expressly refers to it (1972 Constitution, as amended by Law Nº 75-1 of May 1975, Article 32(1); and 1996 Constitution, Article 40). One must note that, as it is the POR himself who must make such express reference, he then becomes the 'law' in the constitutional provisions in question. Is there not clearly the alter ego incomprehensibility here? It is clearly absurd for the POR to be the sole judge of whether or not the Constitution has been violated by legislation (justifying his role as the Chief Justice?), especially as he is the sole legislator. It is only elementary that where the POR, as Anyangwe notes:

> has himself promulgated a law or issued a decree or an ordinance, it is hard to see how he can turn around and challenge its constitutionality. What is more, at the moment all pieces of legislation in Cameroon emanate from the government. The President of the Republic legislates by way of ordinances and decrees. Bills tabled before the National Assembly are always Government Bills. They are generally passed with little or no amendments (Anyangwe, 1987: 206).

L'impossibilité n'est pas vraiment camerounaise (The Impossible Never Really Cameroonian)? Is further illustration needed? Then get it impossibly from one of the 'disputes' in the Article 32(1) in question that provides as follows. The CSC has to be called into action by the POR to ascertain the POR's own permanent incapacity to attend to his duties in Article 7(2). The 1996 version is its Article 8(6): with the Constitutional Council taking the place of the CSC. How the 'permanently incapacitated POR' is then to make the express reference to the CSC (or Constitutional Council, as the case may be), God alone knows (why the Dog in Cameroon has replaced him upside-down?). This arrangement raises the same problems that Professor Wade and others canvass concerning the impracticality of having entrenched rights in the British system with its 'dogma of Parliamentary sovereignty' (Wade, 1980: 22; Tremblay, 1993: 86-87). In a similar way, a Cameroonian POR's act or laws cannot bind his successor. This then could be the reason why President Biya has openly and officially refused to be bound (but still abiding) by President Ahidjo's 1972 Unitary Constitution. This theory is proffered because Biya's 1996 Constitution still regards Cameroon in Article 68 as 'the Federal State of Cameroon' with 'the Federated States...' Even in 1992, Biya's decree that divided Yaoundé into six *arrondissements* was still talking of *La*

République fédérale du Cameroun (see *Décret № 92/187 du 1er septembre 1992*, as discussed by Boyle, 1996: 617 n.37). Is this not a clean case of the *confuser* getting confused himself by his too many confusing constitutions and/or laws? Is it not a clean case of Killing Legislation with Too Much Legislation?

An informed discussion on constitutional amendments (in chapter 3) beautifully cements this thesis on confusion and non-binding acts; but it also comes out clearly here in another 'dispute' that the Supreme Court has to decide on. This has to do with the 1972 Constitution's Article 10 which is just the same as the 1961 Federal Article 14: with the dispute here concerning any law which the POR himself "considers to be contrary to this Constitution" "under the conditions prescribed by the [president's later unknown] law provided for in Article 32" (1972 Constitution, Article 10; and Federal Constitution, Article 14). By this provision, therefore, if the next 'madder President' 'considers' the former mad President's laws contrary to his own constitution and laws, that ends the matter: and no court can say otherwise, especially as the President alone "shall define the policy of the nation" in Articles 5 & 11 of the 1996 Constitution, as well as decide what is constitutional for his packed numberless court to rubber-stamp. That is why I think that the prohibition in the various constitutions, but particularly Article 7 (*nouveau*) of the 1991 Constitution (*Loi Nº 91/001 du 23 avril portant modification des articles 5, 7, 8, 9, 26, 27 et 34 de la Constitution* (hereinafter 1991 Constitution)), on the interim president's ability or powers to "*modifier ni la Constitution, ni la composition du gouvernement*" (inability to change both constitution and government) is, by the same Constitutions and laws, baseless. The same useless prohibition is found also in Article 106 (*nouveau*) of the 1992 Presidential Elections Law (*Loi Nº 92/010 du 17 septembre 1992 fixant les conditions d'élections et de suppléance à la Présidence de la République*) and in the 1996 Constitution's Article 6 (4) (b).

It has been pointed out that to legislate what cannot be done is effectively not to make law; it is rather to unmake law because legislation that cannot be obeyed serves no end but confusion, fear and chaos (Freedman, 1994:151). Professor Dr Michael Milde of McGill University has also been cited for theorizing that, "without enforcement law tends to lose its binding nature and degenerates into a pious statement of principles detached from the reality" (Dempsey, 2004: 2). Moreover, if 'constitutional justice' is defined as that condition in which citizens may trust their government to uphold certain rights considered inviolable, then one is bound to think that unobstructed judicial review of statutes is only one way of attaining that happy state (Cappelletti, 1991: 2). In other words, a society's stability is assured when utopianism is not rife in the Constitution and the law (Kirkpatrick, 1983: 744). It is not then amazing that a human rights activist in Cameroon has observed that:

> I believe that the duty of the law is to serve the end of justice. The end of justice is poorly served by sacrificing the innocent to earn the applause or the sympathy of the powers that be. To save the innocent is not to condone injustice in our legal set up. To save the innocent is to be able to freely question the integrity of a judge or any such person who does not show that the law is supposed to be blind. To save the innocent is to serve the end of justice; it is to ignore crooked, crass legalism or procedure... And it is to save society itself from shooting itself in the foot (Ndi Chia, 1995).

ADVANCING INEQUALITY IN EQUALITY AND UNKNOWINGLY IMPEACHING THE UNWILLING IMPEACHER?

It seems that when they do talk of the judiciary's impartiality and rule of law, Cameroonian leaders have in mind only that organ's duty of doing justice (if at all) between the citizens inter se; and never between them and the government, nor between any other branch and the executive branch which they incarnate. The all-embracing executive must be revered. Excluding the absence of separation explanation, one wonders where the CSC goes to hide its questionable *Affaire Baninga* decision of (sex) equality when government officials break the law and so forth. It is well known "that democratic liberty must work in the context of equality if it is to be acceptable" (Laski, 1950: v). The Constitution that Cameroon's Apex Court is purportedly upholding in its dubious *Affaire Baninga* decision merely very vaguely states that "all persons shall have equal rights and obligations... [and] the State shall guarantee all citizens of either sex the rights and freedoms set forth in the Preamble of the Constitution" (1996 Constitution, Preamble). This means that no one shall stand above the law and Canada appears to show the way here as I demonstrated in the next section.

Equality rights are provided for in Section 15 of the 1982 *Canadian Charter of Rights and Freedom.*(see *The Canadian Charter of Rights and Freedoms*, Part I of the *Constitution Act, 1982*, being Schedule B to the *Canada Act 1982* (U.K.), 1982, c.11). This Section 15 is in two parts. The first guarantees equality before and under the law and the equal protection and benefit of the law, without discrimination, to every individual. The second part specifies that the first part does not preclude affirmative action programs, the purpose of which is to ameliorate the condition of disadvantaged individuals or groups (Iacobucci, 1994: 100). This Section 15 of the Canadian Charter is said to be the Canadian equivalent of the Equal Protection Clause of the 14th Amendment of the American Constitution (ibid: 100-101). Justice Frank Iacobucci offers an incisive comparison of the enactments of these two neighbouring states. An important case turning on the American Clause is *University of California Regents v Bakke* 438 U.S. (1977) 265, in which some critics seem to see only "the most rigid rhetoric of color-blindness" exhibited by Justice Lewis F. Powell who was "in many ways undercutting himself with what must be interpreted as an implicit invitation to hypocritical practice" (Freeman, 1982: 101). This is what the CSC also did in the *Affaire Baninga* case in which it struck down a customary rule of child custody for favouring the deceased's brother against the mother of said children because written law guarantees equality to the sexes. I find it to be hypocritical because an expert has shown that the marriage in question was customary and not supposed to be governed by 'written law' (the Bertoua Court of Appeal being correct in its ruling); but even more so because the CSC has never thereafter applied the sex equality principle across the board: especially when a citizen group is pitted against the state regarding the countless discriminatory provisions in the laws of the land (Fossungu, 2018a: 132-38).

Cameroon's system is an inversion of reality. Quite apart from legal provisions, one can again cite a graphic Policy-Book example of being particularly sex-discriminating at the very time as 'advocating' equality: "It is necessary to make every Cameroonian feel that he is fundamentally equal to all other Cameroonians" (Biya, 1986: 37). The experts must be surprised by the fact that females are excluded ab initio from equality in Cameroon. Why should one then be talking of equality? This is actually what has led some equality rights experts like Brodsky and Day (1989) to posit that it is cleanly a case of one step forward and hundred back. A lot of the critics are also wondering how this Cameroonian feeling of equality can even be brought about when there is open and deliberate second-classing, antagonizing and assimilation of English-speaking Cameroonians: the direct reason for the current schools and lawyers imbroglio bisecting the 'West Cameroon' region.

There is as well the glaring case of one of President Biya's top ministers (currently the Sultan of Foumban – Ibrahim Mbombo Njoya) who shamelessly told Anglophones, when they requested the government to look into their specific concerns, that "*Si vous n'etes pas contents ici, allez ailleurs!*"(Dinga, 1997). If you don't like it here as it is, then leave! This kind of declaration, coming from such a person, is particularly divisive – especially if one also realizes, as narrated by Professor Willard Johnson, that the Bamoum (the current Sultan's father and other influential dignitaries from that ethnic group) played a significant role in bringing the then 'rocking' and elusive reunification of the two Cameroons to reality in Foumban (see Johnson, 1970: 55 & 183-85). In brief, the list of the anti-people acts and utterances of the Biya regime can simply go on and on and on and on. Joe S. Dinga has given a lot of them, including the calling of English-speaking Cameroonians 'the enemies in the house'. All this would not be tolerated in the presence of an independent judiciary. A dependent judiciary like Cameroon's is thus not part of the definition of democracy; hence, not one that can be the bulwark between the state and citizens' rights and freedoms. The dependent judiciary's definition comes out very clearly in the words of Sir Winston Churchill, made during a debate in the British Parliament concerning salaries of judges, as cited in Fossungu (2013b: 142).

To talk of rule of law and judicial impartiality in Cameroon in the absence of a balanced Constitution is like saying a corpse can consume food by the mere fact that food is put near it. Or, that the country's President can actually be impeached simply because there is some scanty provision for a Court of Impeachment in the president's confusion-charged Constitution.

Cameroonian heads of state and of government must still "guard" the independence of the judiciary, expecting all Cameroonians to seriously believe at all times that something awful is going to happen to them if they follow the example of nearly every other country in the world by instituting genuine judicial independence and freedoms and rights of the people. This is what the authorities would actually have in mind when they make the conspicuous declaration of Cameroon having its own specificity not good for borrowed rules (Biya, 1986: 13). An extensive critique of the tumbu-tumbu stance involved here is proffered by Fossungu (2018a: 165-68). Hence, while other judiciaries have been progressively growing in strength with age and constitutional amendments such as the 1974 amendment of the

Supreme Court Act in Canada, as neatly discussed by Professor Wade (1980: 71), Cameroon's 'judicial power' has been doing just the reverse since until today (one cannot be wrong to just say that) it simply does not exist.

THE FEDERAL HIGH COURT OF JUSTICE: AN IMPEACHMENT INSTITUTION?

Cameroon's advanced democracy will nevertheless raise objection to all this, indicating how there was even a Federal High Court of Justice (FHCJ) with jurisdiction over high officials of the federation and of the states in cases of high treason and/or conspiracy against the security of the state – that is, the entire federal republic (Federal Constitution, Article 36). One can be tempted to say that the FHCJ was a court of impeachment. This court was taken up mot-a-mot by the 1972 Constitution's Article 34 but the 1984 Constitution's Article 34(1) adopted it only to a limited extent. This is now the 1996 Constitution's Article 53 that is to be discussed shortly. Another law promulgated in 1991, as the advanced democratic argument would proceed, also created 'a high court of justice whose functioning and organization will be determined by a later law' – *"une haute cour de justice dont les conditions de saisir et l'organisation seront déterminées par la loi"* (1991 Constitution, Article 34 (*nouveau*)). That is actually what the specialists brand as 'framed legislation' and readers could get its significance in the loose translation of this other provision of the 1996 Constitution's Article 42(1): "The organization, functioning, composition and duties of the Supreme Court and the benches it comprises, the conditions for referring matters to them as well as the procedure applicable before them shall be laid down by law.

THE 1991 AND 1996 HIGH COURTS OF JUSTICE IMPEACHING THE PRESIDENT

The 1991 Constitution's French-only Article 34 (*nouveau*) is actually confusingly saying that a High Court of Justice has been created but the conditions regulating it, etc, are to be laid down by a subsequent 'higher law' which, of course, in Professor Anyangwe's pertinent words, is "often a presidential decree or a ministerial order. Also, it sometimes happens that laws are so hurriedly [and secretly] drafted that no sooner have they rolled out of the printing press than there are amendments" (cited in Fossungu, 2013b: 144). The new 1991 Court of Impeachment had, as its jurisdiction, *"pour juger les actes accomplis dans l'exercice de leurs fonctions par le Président de la République en cas de haute trahison et par le Premier Ministre, les ministres, les secrétaires d'état et les responsables de l'administration ayant reçu délégation de pouvoir, en application de l'article 5 ci-dessus en cas de complot contre la sûreté de l'état"* – 1991 Constitution, Article 34 (*nouveau*)). Well, to legitimately corrupt it with my unauthentic translation, here is what the New Article 34 is authentically saying: "to judge the President of the Republic for high treason [who defines what this is? Only the POR himself knows], the Prime Minister, secretaries of state and other high-ranking state officials for conspiracy against state security." That is exactly how constitutional Cameroon is, the advanced democrats will constitutionally conclude to prospective importers of the confusioncracy.

But is that real or just a 'paper system' designed solely to confuse prospective buyers? Are legal and constitutional principles respected by all the parties, without exception such that no one (including the president) stands above the law? Talking about the law applying even to the POR, it must be recalled that former President Amadou Ahidjo was tried and sentenced in absentia for attempting (on 6 April 1984) against the security and integrity of the State. This trial, one is inclined to think, was only possible because Ahidjo was then no longer president. His trial, moreover, cannot even be correctly termed impeachment – since the conditions (of *les actes accomplish dans l'exercice de leurs fonctions*) in Article 34 (*nouveau*) cannot have been met. Could the Cameroonian president ever have been tried at all while in office: as *almost* happened to President William Jefferson Clinton in the United States? Brownstein (1998) has handled the American case, competently exploding some impeachment myths, whose detonation is unthinkable in Cameroon? One can only answer this graphical question by looking at the case of the current Cameroonian President.

In addition to the regime's outbursts described above, President Biya's new 1996 Constitution, with all its divisive and yet-to-be-defined concepts would properly fall under 'acts committed in the exercise of their functions' to actually warrant "The [President's new] Court of Impeachment... to try the President of the Republic for high treason and... for conspiracy against the security of the State" (1996 Constitution, Article 53(1)). That must have to be the case, if 'State' in this constitutional provision means anything other than the POR. But then it is not known how anyone can ever impeach the Cameroonian emperor-president when, like its predecessors, "the organization, composition and the conditions under which matters shall be referred to it [court of impeachment] as well as the procedure applicable before the Court of Impeachment shall be laid down by [the POR's subsequent] law" (1996 Constitution,

Article 53(2)). And who, apart from the same POR to be tried, is similarly going to decree how such judgments (including even those of the Military Tribunal in Yaoundé) are to be executed? This particular query finds its legitimacy in the following unilingual pieces of legislation: *Loi Nº 89/020 du 29 décembre 1989 fixant certaines disposition relatives à l'exécution des décisions de justice*; *Ordonnance Nº 97/01 du 04 mai 1997 modifiant les articles 3 et 4 de la Loi Nº 92/080 du 14 aout 1992 fixant certaines dispositions relative à l'exécution des décisions de justice*; and *Loi Nº 97/018 du 07 aout 1997 modifiant les articles 3 et 4 de la Loi Nº 92/008 du 14 aout 1982 fixant certaines dispositions relative à l'exécution des décisions de justice*. Also, important to the point is the Military Justice Law of January 1997 (see *Loi Nº 97/008 du 10 janvier modifiant certaines dispositions de l'ordonnance Nº 72/5 du 26 aout 1972 portant organisation judiciaire militaire*). Of what value then is the Court of Impeachment except as the POR's instrument of oppressing everyone, including even his cronies? It is thus highly doubtful that even the defunct Federal Court of Justice (FCJ) lived up to any of its glorious duties, especially as its composition and procedure (as well as those of any other court) and the rules under which cases were to be brought before the FCJ were also the subject of a later unknown 'higher law' (see Federal Constitution, Article 33(4)).

CONCLUDING WITH PLACES TO LEARN FROM

The case of Germany (to spare Canada some over work) may be important here for emulation. The German judicial branch that is charged with justice administration is laid down with some specific rules right there in the Constitution known as Basic Law and not left as the subject of later executive laws. (See Basic Law for the Federal Republic of Germany in the revised version published in the Federal Law Gazette Part III, classification number 100-1, as last amended by the Act of 29 July 2009 (Federal Law Gazette I p. 2248)). Chapter IX of the Basic Law (Articles 92-104) elaborately covers the Administration of Justice, with the following being especially important to bring out for emulation in Cameroon and other African states. The German judicial power is well treated in the Basic Law (Article 92), with the independence of judges being guaranteed in Article 97; the jurisdiction of the Federal Constitutional Court and its composition are all provided for right there in the Basic Law's Articles 93 and 94. So too are the Supreme Federal courts, the exercise of federal jurisdiction by courts of the Lander and the status of Federal and Land judges in Articles 96 and 98. Both Bothe (1991) and Orban (1991) would furnish further discussion of the matter.

Belgium adds some uniqueness to this. Another unique aspect of the Belgian Court's composition, reflecting the lingering fears of 'a Government by the Judiciary', is the fact that six of the judges must be former parliamentarians not necessarily possessing legal training or qualifications. Early commentators, while aware of the harmful potential of renewing old political quarrels thereby, were generally favourable to the idea, emphasizing that the control of the constitutionality of laws is a way of partaking in the exercise of political power: *'le contrôle de la constitutionalité des loi est une forme de participation au pouvoir politique'* (Shapiro, 1995: 67-68). The idea of filling the courts with non-lawyers has been trenchantly criticized by both Radamaker (1987: 129-52) and Shapiro (1995: 68). The judicial institution (no matter how staffed) does not participate in political power in any form whatsoever in Cameroon. Here the POR, and that President alone, has always had the yam and knife, the cloth and the sewing machine. People who think that it was otherwise with the Federal Constitution must then have to explicate why, for instance, President Amadou Ahidjo was not impeached for his so-called 1972 'coup d'état upon Cameroon,' that is, his personal 'transformation' of the Federal Republic of Cameroon into a highly centralized unitary state – United Republic of Cameroon, now simply without 'united' since President Biya's 1984 Constitution that sparked off secessionist drives (or what is now popularly known as the *Anglophone Problem*) in Cameroon.

In a situation of genuine and effective federalism, all this could not have happened without a momentous ruling from independent courts. It is thus only independent courts that can also authoritatively ordain that the 1972 Constitution was "the embodiment of the most significant of ... manipulations [by] ... which Cameroonians were made to opt for a unitary state and this has gone down in history as the most significant date in the political history of Cameroon" (Mensah-Gbadago,1991: 4). Neither would what is now happening at the western side of the Mungo River not already have received the ruling of courts in Cameroon. Federalism proper is the solution to the national unity crisis in Cameroon in particular and Africa in general, not being something to be "authorized" by an individual but to be undertaken by the determined peoples and regions of this country or continent. What aggravates the situation in Cameroon is that the overwhelming majority of French-speaking Cameroonians have been brainwashed to view federalism as the synonym of secession, with the false idea being fortified to be almost right by the 'conflicting' and 'opportunistic' narratives from the Anglophone elites or "intellectuals in politics" as already noted above. The next chapter studies the role played in the judicial independence discourse by the recruitment and training processes of lawyers, judges, magistrates and teachers.

CHAPTER 2

JUDICIAL INDEPENDENCE AND THE MAKING OF TEACHERS, JUDGES AND LAWYERS IN AFRICA: *CASE OF CAMEROON*

A credible legal profession (bench, bar, and academia) is an indispensable part of the judicial independence message. During the June 1996 inaugural dinner of the nascent Common Law Society of Cameroon that was attended by some 90 Anglophone lawyers in Limbe in Debundschazone of Cameroon, Charles Twining (then United States Ambassador to Cameroon) reminded the "lawyers that an independent judiciary and respect for human rights were the fundamental basis of democracy" (Sunde, 1996: 3). Can anyone then hope to find Mr and Mrs Justice Legality Fairness (or even the Royal Road leading to their place of abode) anywhere in a society with ignorant self-centred and money-chasing lawyers as those in Cameroon? Of course, occasionally, these professionals around the globe do forget the people; but their Cameroonian friends seem not to just forget but actually actively brutalize the people that they are supposed to be protecting. Attorney General Janet Reno of the United States told us in 1994 that, because of their over belief in the written word, "American lawyers have forgotten and neglected the people. They have become too taken with the process, with the form and with the written word and they have not remembered the heart, the soul, the spirit, and the intellect that lies behind the people they represent"(Reno, 1994: 8; also see Williams, 1987: 401-403) Some experts have attributed the sorrowful trend to "the[ir] hot pursuit of happiness" (Cairns, 1990: viii).

Like the American lawyers, Cameroonian lawyers also hotly pursue 'happiness': the sole difference being in their doing so largely, if not exclusively, for the stomach and without the law – a body of regulations which is supposed, normally, to be in their safe keeping. In discussing their 'Money Making' (Anyangwe, 1989: 119-120), an expert came to the pathetic conclusion that "[w]riting of articles of legal interest (or even writing in general) is something the Cameroonian advocate never indulges in. The Cameroonian Bar itself runs no legal periodical. It maintains a conspiratorial silence on such issues as law reform and human rights in Cameroon" (ibid: 120 n.44). Lawyers are everywhere considered to be the 'Masters of the Word', 'the law givers', the 'Prideful Lions that leadeth the flocking sheep', etc. Do those in Cameroon meet these descriptions to be able to shape the direction in justice administration? Not really; hence the unwarrantable legalization of inhuman rights and injustice administration in this blessed (but now cursed) African country called Cameroon.

The plain fact is that the quality of justice in any society largely depends on the calibre of people on its bench and bar. The ideal conclusion of experts like Elhrich is that justice is an alloy of judges and mechanisms in which the judges count more than machinery. Assume the clearest rules, the most enlightened procedures, and the most sophisticated court techniques the key factor is still the judge (Rosenburg, 1973: 1). This could explain why former Tanzanian President, Julius Nyerere, told Judges and Resident Magistrates at Arusha on 15 March 1984 that "there are jobs which can be done by undisciplined people and people whose personal integrity can be called into question; being a Judge or Magistrate is not among them" (Wambali and Peter, 1987: 131). According to an expert on Cameroon's Magistracy and Bar:

> In order to ensure the good administration of justice every system has a double task; on the one hand to establish a system of guarantees that will ensure the independence of the judges, and on the other hand to develop a system of rules governing the recruitment of judges that will ensure that the candidates selected have both the necessary technical (legal expertise,

forensic and human experience, intelligence and commonsense) and moral qualities. Both are two sides of the same coin. The method of recruitment of judges is in itself an essential factor in the personal independence of the judge (Anyangwe, 1989: 8).

Stason (1973: 46) completely agrees with Anyangwe here. Because of the important role that the judiciary plays in ensuring respect for the rule of law and the smooth functioning of federalism, one of the reform proposals from Professor Fombad of the University of Pretoria is that judicial appointments and recruitment in Cameroon should be depoliticised by using appointment committees with less than half of their members having any links, whether directly or indirectly, to the executive and the legislature (Fombad, 2014: 448). All these would form part of the rules, procedures and techniques; but what are the required qualities for good justiceships then? Lord Denning, in his *The Road to Justice* (1955), generally attempts an elaborate cataloguing of the qualities of a good judge. But Professor Rosenburg simply finds the composition of a list of these qualities "notoriously elusive" and "particularly obscure when the qualities sought are personal, subjective, and human," which makes the problem "a vexing one" (Rosenburg, 1973: 2 & 6). This vexing problem is aggravated in

Cameroon by the mode of recruiting and training judges, lawyers, teachers and other public servants.

In addition to both entrance and training of lawyers to be seen shortly, the (judicial and legal) profession in Cameroon is male-dominated, with mainly young single people within the 28-40 years age group who lack the courage, boldness and initiative required of the job (Anyangwe, 1989: 4-5 & chapter 11). It is not surprising then that cases such as judges and magistrates and lawyers having sex and financial scandals are very frequent in Cameroon (see Fossungu, 2013b; 147). These matters are actually bound together but one will try to separate them as far as can be possible just for convenience in this chapter that has three main parts. The first demonstrates the political naivety or idiocy of Cameroonian political and legal elites which would be directly tied to concentration of powers and/or their useless colonial education, especially from the so-called professional schools. The second handles the 'competitive exams' or *concours* as a recruitment and training method, the third examines how one becomes a practising lawyer in Cameroon which has no law school, including the available facilities for the continuing education and update of teachers, judges and magistrates and lawyers

WONDERS NEVER ENDING WITH POLITICAL IDIOTS: SUBVERTING SEPARATION OF POWERS BY PENAL-CODING SEPARATION OF POWERS?

With or without federalism, Cameroon clearly inverts countries like Canada since (1) administrative and/or constitutional litigation is/are still absent in Cameroon because of the absence of separation of powers, which also means (2) that the courts have no control over constitutional amendments (see chapter 3 for more on amendments). Interestingly, in this African country, all this has been achieved, thanks also to the confusioncratic strategy of subverting separation of powers by Penal-Coding separation of powers. The separation of powers doctrine is subverted not only through the numerous confusing constitutions in Cameroon. The country's so-called 'Model Penal Code for Africa' (according to Professor J.A. Clarence Smith (1968): 671) denies it as well. "No discussion of the doctrine of separation of powers", one expert on Cameroon constitutional law has tersely warned, "is complete without mention of sections 125, 126, and 127 of Book II of the Cameroon Penal Code" (Enonchong, 1967: 103).

Found in Chapter II of said Book II of the CPC, all these sections deal with what is called 'Trespass [on

Jurisdiction]'. Section 125 which is captioned 'On Legislature' states: "Any public servant who – (a) Assumes the exercise of legislative powers; or (b) Refuses to enforce any provision of law – shall be punished with detention for from six months to five years." Section 126 is titled 'By Executive and Judiciary reciprocally' and ordains that: "Whoever – (a) Being the representative of the executive authority, issues any order or prohibition to any court; or (b) Being a legal or judicial officer, issues any order or prohibition to any executive or administrative authority – shall be punished with detention for from six months to five years." According to Dr Carlson Anyangwe's sane interpretation of this provision, "Their [judges'] job" in Cameroon, "is merely to apply the [President's] law and to show no creativity. Even when construing an obscure statute they are not entitled 'to make any far-fetched interpretation of the law or justice'" (Anyangwe, 1989: 25). Fossungu (1997) offers a more extensive critique of this particular anti-libertarian formula The third provision (Section 127) is captioned 'by Judiciary on Particular Immunities' and mandates that "Any judicial, legal or investigating police officer who, contrary to any law conferring immunity prosecutes, arrests or tries a member of the federal or a federated Government, or of the federal or federated Assembly, shall be punished with detention for from one to five years." There is certainly a lot more to be said of this so-called Model Penal Code for Africa, but let's see or imagine what curious combination this arrangement has with the remuneration and qualities (and, therefore, independence) of judges and of the country's politicians.

THE QUESTIONS OF CAMEROON POLITICIANS AND LAWYERS: EVIDENCE OF ILLITERACY OR CONFUSIONCRACY?

All these penal sections and many more, while conspicuously claiming to be separating powers, only go to ensure that judges are not independent and remain mere automatons. As all these pieces of legislation and other constitutional provisions are still in place and applying, it then beats the imagination of anyone who takes the issues seriously that the bulk of Cameroonian intellectuals – claiming to be out there after democracy – are *only* rushing to create political parties and run for public office, including even the presidency, without first making sure that the country's Supreme Court in particular and the journalists were in a comfortable position to perform the duties that democracy necessarily exacts from them. As a well-meaning journalist has fascinatingly put it to these bellyticians, "[d]emocracy cannot thrive when the press is *squared* and journalists victimized. Democracy cannot thrive when gendarmes are constantly drafted and given the leeway to sack university campuses, assault scholars, [and] loot property and *poach* the womanhood of Daughters of Eve... Democracy does not thrive when writers of international repute are jailed, parcel-bombed or slaughtered" (Ndi Chia, 1995: 4, original omission & emphasis). Osofisan (1996: 11-14) has also harped on the wanton jailing and slaughtering of writers of international repute.

How then are the myriad of opposition leaders and the lawyers in Cameroon really committed to genuine change? This question has to be asked again and again because it is believed that anyone truly out for the necessary changes that Cameroon badly needs to terminate the bloodbath going on in the country cannot only be rushing to form useless political parties to run for the presidency without having first made sure there was a credible referee for the game. It appears, therefore, to be just about bellytics (or belly politics), not change to these people. To adopt Fossungu's (2013a: 138) fitting questioning: "Shouldn't any right-thinking person have first made sure that this [country's] un-supreme court becomes effectively supreme before launching into creating a political party?" Otherwise, I would like to go on and add, does it not merely become a case of trying to force out (if they even could do so without arms in the Laurent-Kabila manner) the incumbent dictator only to assume that same dictator position?

Yet, these same politicians (bellyticians, to be accurate) expect miracles from the caged Supreme Court when they come to its portals for redemption of rights! The *Bouba Bello* case begins illustrating the nasty folly. As reported by Abel Eyinga, Bello challenged a decree by which the POR appointed government delegates to localities won by other political parties whereas nowhere in his constitution is there provision for that. The chained Supreme Court of Cameroon, since declaring that the complaint from Mr. Bello was founded, went into an inexplicable total silence, for close to two years, on the issue of actually hearing the case and rendering a verdict. Why?[1] Does the mere asking of the question here not very succinctly expose their political naivety that has been excellently shown by some experts like Fossungu (2018a) to be very promotional of the poverty and deprivation that Africa is now well known for?

---

[1] *"Je crois savoir qu'il y a à peu près deux ans Bello Bouba [le président de l'UNDP] avait saisi la cour suprême au sujet de décret en question en disant que ce décret va contre la loi. La Cour suprême a reconnu que ce recours de Bello Bouba était recevable. Et depuis, elle n'a plus rien fait, c'est le silence total. Alors pourquoi la Cour ne juge pas?"* (Eyinag, 1996 : 7).

This country's self-centred and divided lawyers too *only* talk the constitution and human rights in selected instances. That is, only when one or all of them would have been affected such as the 'Poorest-ugliest French bijuralism' & 'bilingualism in French' that Reverend Gerald Jumban says is directly behind the current crisis in 'Anglophone Cameroon' (or what is now known as Ambazonia):

> I wish to let you know something of the people of the Southern Cameroons which many French Speaking Cameroonians seem to be ignorant of. They are people who do not distinguish between their love of country and their love of the Church. They love those two things with their whole hearts. Their patriotism is ethical, concrete, and religiously dutiful - reason why your brother bishops of Southern Cameroons (in the example of that pragmatic culture) have spoken for their subjugated and dispossessed people against such a stinking political tyranny as Biya's. That is why though many from East Cameroon are comfortable with the atheistic political system glorifyingly baptized laicité, it has been scandal of the highest order to the religious sensitivity of Southern Cameroons who like true Africans (and tinged by Anglicanism's reverence for God and respect for the Monarch) believe that without God and indigenous

culture life is impossible. We know very well that this atheism we see in Cameron politics is not from your own ancestors but it is borrowed from France. The people East of the Mungo have been educated in Gallican opinions. We of the West have been educated in Anglican opinions. The respect of each other's opinions from those educational systems have been what La République du Cameroun has deprived us of, and it pains us to the marrow. That is why our teachers and lawyers took to the streets to peacefully demonstrate their anger and protest against an evil system. They were met with an autocratic response by a government you fear to criticize" (Jumbam, 2017).

In such a case affecting them, these lawyers will even go as far as threatening or frightening the helpless judicial official with: "Let justice and liberty triumph... You [the judge] are facing the challenge of Cameroon history today. You are called upon to deliver a juridico-political decision. Do not forget that Paul Biya is a politician; has he the power to divide this nation?" They were making all these incomprehensible demands in this local newspaper piece – titled "The Regime in Question is the CPDM" in *Cameroon Post* of 20-25 May 1990 on pages 5-8 – reporting the trial of Maitre Yondo Mandengue Black and Ten Others by the Military Tribunal in Yaoundé for attempting to create a political party. *Yondo et al* is also reported in Brody (1990: 15). The shortest answer to these lawyers' blinkered question is YES. But some experts would prefer to simply say that, as "[e]verything in this country is changing [for the worse], it's in the air... We don't have any answers; we only have some questions and a deep desire to talk" (Schneiderman, 1992: 5, citing Lee Maracle).

These deep desires to talk and the questions concern especially the education of Cameroon's elites. When lawyers (of all professionals in a society) do find nothing wrong in constitutions that expressly exclude the judiciary from the exercise of political power in Article 4 as well as making the POR (Paul Biya) the guarantor of that institution's independence in Article 37, one should then wonder what to make of their subsequently making these demands of a judge of that same institution. Is it illiteracy or confusioncracy? We also conspicuously see their friends of the academy also asking the same judges to boldly construe the same constitution without themselves standing firm and creatively demonstrating to the judges (as is expected) just how the judges should go about doing so. All this can only usher in the legitimate doubts of some critics as to whether the idea of ethical and radical lawyering is merely oxymoronic in its expression or actually moronic in its aspiration (Hutchinson, 1995: 768). How on earth could judicial independence (that guarantees justice in governance) ever have found a place in a society with such lawyers?

Judicial and constitutional rhetoric would obviously provide the most appropriate channels for answering or solving important human rights questions such as those still plaguing Cameroon as we speak. Children in the English-speaking part of the country have been out of school for close to four years now and there is no likelihood that the situation would be arrested any time soon. Yet, no court has been seen to have passed judgment on the question, since it is clear that judicial rhetoric in particular can hardly exist in the absence of judicial independence. Separation of powers is meaningless in Cameroon where one-sentence judgments of one-man unijural and unilingual courts do reign supreme. The Douala courts (representative of 'East Cameroun' – and, therefore, the entire Cameroonian (see Fossungu, 2018a)) – version of injustice administration) are noted for being places in which a litigant with a plain and clear case often fervently prays "their Lordships to declare that justice was on his side of the disputation. [But o]ne by one their Lordships turned him down sometimes with one sentence judgements. His lawyer screamed that the Douala decision amounted to judicial harlotry [saying] that justice was only available to [those] who could pay for it" (Ndi Chia, 1995: 4). As some specialists have indicated, all this would scarcely be unanticipated to anyone who knows Cameroon as a place "filled to the brim with abhorrent laws that even punish a judge for rendering justice" (Fossungu, 2013b: 26). All that state-sponsored injustice administration would come out more clearly as the recruitment and training of judicial and legal and other public officials in Cameroon are closely inspected, a process that seems to be solely directed mainly at curbing judicial independence.

THE 'CONCOURS' AS RECRUITMENT AND TRAINING MODALITY

Entrance into and training at Cameroon's National Administration and Magistracy School (ENAM) are fraudulent and questionable. Just imagine a guy on the bench who got there by bribing his way there and the entire sorrowful tale (of 'justice being available to only those who can pay for it') has already been told almost completely. But let's still tell it, taking the first aspect first. In addition to being mono-cultural, entrance to Cameroon's Civil-Law-only professional schools (including ENAM for judges and magistrates) is, in the first place, hardly based on excellence and fitness for the job. The gapping absence of administrative and other litigation in Cameroon is also heavily tied to these wanting features. Discussing 'The Pathology of the Administrative System' (Anyangwe, 1996: 824-25), Dr Carlson Anyangwe reached the conclusion that "the vast majority of complaints are from public servants, basically those in the top bracket which is category 'A' – with those in the lower brackets being generally indifferent to the violation of their rights or unaware of the fact that the administration can be sued for wrongs" (ibid: 824).

The reason behind this indifference is not hard to find. Some critics like Aseh (1996: 3) have also tied it to the bottlenecks in Cameroon that are solely designed to make people desperate and thus accept just anything. Added to that is the pathetic condition of Cameroon's teachers (including those of the law) who are supposed to be involved in the 'militant and constant warfare' of teaching Cameroonians about their most basic rights. Teaching, according to a Canadian education expert, is:

what I [have] just called a militant enterprise, a constant warfare. The really dangerous battlefront is not the one against ignorance, because ignorance is to some degree curable. It is the battlefront against prejudice and malice, the attitude of people who cannot stand the thought of a fully realized humanity, of human life without the hysteria and panic that controls every moment of their own lives. Words like 'elitism' become for such people bogey words used to describe those who try to take their education seriously (Frye, 1986: 31).

It is not exactly clear how on earth ignorant and hungry teachers, filled to the brim with hypocrisy, can be as militant as the nature of their calling demands. Some critics have narrated how Cameroonian teachers' "visible pain, desperation, estrangement and their hypocrisy reminds a regular church-goer about the Bible stories of the Israelites in the wide wilderness separating them from the distant and receding promise land" (Fohtung, 1996). Barry Fohtung's theory is supported by contributions from Francophhone juornalists such as Atenga (1997) and Kidane (1997). It is then not astonishing that their students (now aggrieved public servants and who hardly know their rights vis-à-vis the state) are timorous and refrain from taking on the administration for fear of subsequent persecution by the latter: loss of increment or promotion, arbitrary salary cuts, suspension of salary, delay in the payment of salary, transfer to a remote part of the country, demotion or even dismissal (Anyangwe, 1996: 825; Fombad, 2014: 436-37).

Another factor said to be responsible for the poverty in administrative litigation in Cameroon is the fact that it is essentially a public service affair, with the vast majority of suits being from them. Most of these complaints are about career problems, disciplinary matters and tax issues and would "clearly suggest that administrative litigation operates as a closed circuit, as an internal organ of the administration itself, again confirming the concept of the administrative litigation as a mere justice déléguée" (Anyangwe, 1996: 824). What these critics are saying here is cemented by Supreme and/or Appeal Court decisions such as "the Public Service minister has clearly violated the decree in question but no damages can be made to the aggrieved party"! ("*le Ministre de la Fonction Publique a violé les dispositions de l'art 131 du décret Nº 74/138... mais la demande d'allocation de dommages-intérêt est rejetée.*" That is coming from *CS/CA, Jugement Nº 38/89-90 du 31 mai 1990: sieur Ndoudoumou Nkili Jean c Etat du Cameroun (MFPCE)* – reported by Professeur Maurice Kamto in 1992 in 10 *Juridis Info (Revue de Législation et de Jurisprudence Camerounaises)* 52 at 53). In addition, almost all the contested administrative decisions emanate from the central authority; being a clear indication that administrative litigation "is practically confined to the capital city and that the administrative system is ultra-centralised (what is known in the literature as *le jacobinisme unitaire,* that is Jacobean unitarism or extreme centralisation)" (Anyangwe, 1996:

824). It is only obvious that, in a system like this one, most, if not all, of such claims are "mundane and do not call for any judicial creativity. The work of the [Cameroon] administrative court is therefore routine and dull" (ibid).

Some education experts like Simon Nkwenti have found Cameroon teachers' knowledge to be very thinly different from that of those they are to be teaching (Fossungu, 2013a: 180). Even teachers from "the dubious *Ecoles Normales*" (Barry Fohtung's words), especially the Anglophone ones, have always to abandon school children for weeks and months in order to make the usual 'pilgrimage' to the 'Super-Market' Ministry of Finance in Yaoundé in view of "bribing and 'screwing' their way to integration in Yaoundé's civil service or towards their meagre salary arrears" (Fohtung, 1996: 8). But these same instructors are the first to recoil in the usual predictable way "when it comes to the Anglophone Problem or, say, *decentralization which can spare them the costly trips to Yaoundé*" (ibid, emphasis added). This obviously would also explain why these 'running-nose' civil servants, according to another expert:

Had refused to join the wagon of change, arguing: *Mon salaire passe: où est mon problème...* because, at the time, Mother France was still willing to back [defeated Francophone] Biya [against victorious Anglophone Ni

John Fru Ndi] by paying the civil service. This could only mean that (1) as long as everything is fine with them here and now, why do they have to bother about their children? [A]nd (2) they would have joined in the struggle to effectively bring down the system only if their 'privilege' (that is the way this bunch of contradictory uncivilized civil servants consider their salary) did not flow. The gathering storm [from the *villes mortes* or ghost towns] was, consequently, not strong enough to do the job.

Now, what has happened to the passing and even to the thing that used to pass? The ball has changed court. It is now the turn of these civil servants. The first thing they salute you with these days is always '*mon salaire*' that has been slashed into ten... and even the tenth he or she cannot get at the end of the month. And they will even be announcing [this] to you, expecting sympathy on your part! (cited in Fossungu, 2015a: 101)

All this is not unexpected especially viewing the questionable manner of recruiting and training these civil servants. What Professor Rosenburg (1973: 3) condemns it as "looking for lawyers with copybook virtues" could be likened to what the Nigerian movie industry (Nollywood) is constantly mocking as "charge and bail lawyers." In Cameroon, even the vexing laid down "mere book intelligence" or "paper qualification" criteria to the total exclusion of moral rectitude, etc. (Anyangwe, 1989: 4, 9, & 8) are never even adhered to; having been utterly displaced by the deplorable "god-fathering" and "man-know-man" and other such corruption instruments. Fossungu (2013a: 178-82) has catalogued some of them. Entrance into ENAM, like all similar professional schools, is by the infamous *concour* (governed by *Décret Nº 90/1087 du 25 juin 1990 fixant le régime général des concours administratifs*: enacted in view of *Décret Nº 74/138 du 18 février 1974 portant statut général de la Fonction Publique* (hereinafter Concours Decree)). These *concours* are of four categories. The Concours Decree classes them as follows: (1) *concours directs* are governed by Chapter I (Articles 6-10), (2) *concours professionnels* are detailed out in Chapter II (Articles 11-14), (3) *concours speciaux* come under Chapter III (Articles 15-19), and (4) *concours de bourse de formation ou de perfectionnement* are the province of Chapter IV (Article 20). These *concours* are announced by the Minister of Public Service (Article 3(1)) although the organization of those not specifically aimed at training people exclusively for the civil service can be announced by the "*Ministre de tutelle desdits établissements, à condition que le Ministre chargé de la Fonction Publique y soit associé*" (Article 3(2)). Its Articles 21-58 are concerned with the organization of *concours* in Cameroon. The different programmes of these *concours* (which consist of the written, oral, and an eventual practical, parts [2]) are regulated by "*des arrêtes*" of the Public Service Minister, with the proposal of the other concerned ministers (Article 4). Readers should not be offended that most of the provisions are in their original French because it makes the point better that Cameroon is pure and pure a Unilingual 'bilingual' country only to the English-speaking. "Bilingual in French" is how some Quebec University professors have aptly described it (see Benjamin, 1972).

All magistrates are in category 'A', although one must also bear in mind that each of these categories is further broken down into, say, B1, B2... All civil servants in Cameroon are categorized and scaled; with these scales and categories being laid down by further decrees of the President of the Republic. The decree generally governing the judges and their friends of the DPP – Ministère Public – is Decree *№82-467 of 4 October 1982* (otherwise known as *Rules and Regulations of the Judicial and Legal Service*). These *Rules* are appended to Anyangwe's (1989) instructive book on Cameroon's Magistracy and Bar. Law degree holders write these

---

[2] Concours Decree, Article 5. *Concours* for category 'D' posts consist only of the written examination.

concours not only to get into ENAM and become judges and magistrates. The ENAM candidates mostly look to the customs side of administration since that is where it is believed the heftiest bribes are. An undergraduate law degree (LL.B.) in most of Canada outside Quebec is necessarily a second for most students undertaking it, unlike in Cameroon (as well as in Kenya and most English-speaking African countries – see Ojwang and Salter (1989: 82)) where it is most often, if not principally, one's very first degree. This feature is particularly pronounced in Cameroon principally because, strangely enough (and as a consequence of Decree Nº 79/299; and Ministerial Order Nº 194/B1/76/MINEDUC/DES of 11 August 1979), one could not be admitted into any of three University of Yaoundé (UNIYAO) Faculties (of Law and Economics, of Letters and Social Sciences, and of Sciences) once one was twenty-five and above.

Some legal experts think this provision makes Cameroon "probably the only country in the world where being over 25 years of age is a bar to a university education" (Anyangwe, 1989: 198); with yet others 'expibasketically' detailing out the consequences and effects of this 'Age Politics in University Education in Cameroon' (Fossungu, 2013c: chapter 4). It would appear that this issue is what the authorities in Cameroon must have had in mind when they wrote in their Policy-Book in 1986 that "there should be no limit to the people's right to learning" (Biya, 1986: 127). Yet, it is not certain that the 25-year-age-limit bar on university education in Cameroon has been abolished at this moment. As has been duly indicated by some experts (see chapter 3), the inflation of legislation in Cameroon makes it extremely hard to know what law is still applying and which has been repealed and by which; leading to an expert's realistic charge of "Confusioncracy Passing for Balanced Development" (Fossungu, 2013a: 206-224). It is thus not clear if the above age-limit decree and order have been rescinded, but I keep wondering because I am also not sure that the two new so-called 'Anglo-Saxon' universities (in Buea and in Bamenda) are rejecting candidates on the age score. Or are they?

That is not the most important thing here though. The immediate query has to do with corruption. Corruption has eaten so much into the Cameroonian fabric that citizens are even wondering why they should still be paying taxes which would only end up in individual overseas bank accounts especially. Two university lecturers in Cameroon have thus explored how Cameroonians view the payment of taxes to the state in the backdrop of the pervasive corruption and the dismal levels of social service provision characterising public governance in the country since the early 1990s; coming to the conclusion that such negative perceptions about taxation illustrate the challenges confronting African states if they seek to expand their capacity for domestic resource mobilisation through taxation (Orock and Mbuagbo, 2012). One of Professor Charles Manga Fombad's proposals for constitutionalism and progress therefore touches on corruption which he sees as probably the worst cancer, not only destroying the economies of most of the countries in the studied Central African region, but also undermining faith in constitutionalism, especially electoral democracy and respect for the rule of law. He has then suggested that radical anticorruption measures should be constitutionalised, which will render corruption a business in which the risk totally outweighs the benefits (Fombad, 2014: 448). Mbaku (2014b) also shares the same view.

To concretely illustrate the cancer in Cameroon within our topic of discussion, we easily find people 'passing' competitive examinations into professional schools, including ENAM, without even having sat for it or being holders of the first degree (e.g., LL.B., B.A., or BSc.) that is required for taking the examination. It is better to let Damien Fouda Bodo to more elegantly recount it to readers. He talks, for example, of an incident on 21

November 1996 at 3.30 (half past three) in the afternoon, when CRTV/Radio announced the results of the entrance *concours* to the higher teachers-training school (*École Normale Supérieure*, it is called). As soon as the list of the names of those declared successful in the *concours* had been read over radio, wild cries took hold of the student residential quarters (Bonamoussadi) of the University of Yaoundé. What for? Because of what has just been said above in English, being my loose executive transcription of Bodo's: "*Ce ne sont pas des cris de joie, mais d'indignation due au fait que les étudiants reconnaissent les noms de leurs camarades qui n'ont même pas présenté le concours, mais qui ne sont pour autant pas moins admis. Ils constatent aussi que parmi «les élus du jour» beaucoup ne sont pas du tout licenciés; portant la licence est le diplôme exigé pour présenter ce concours*" (Bodo, 1996 : 6). That was as far as getting into the school to become and remain a corrupt magistrate or judge goes. Is the position any different with those law degree holders that want to become professional or practising lawyers? That is what the next section tries to find out.

BECOMING A LAWYER IN CAMEROON WITH NO LAW SCHOOL AND FACILITIES FOR CONTINUING EDUCATION

Law graduates intending to become practising lawyers in Cameroon have to specifically take the bar entrance or *concours* to be able to undertake articling, or what is known in Cameroon as pupilage. The entrance conditions for the bar in Cameroon are governed by *Décret Nº 91/0305 du 4 juillet 1991 relatif à l'examen d'aptitude au stage d'avocat*, and the Internal Regulations of the Bar. "In Cameroon academic education is offered in the Law Faculty of the University of Yaoundé while professional training is under-taken in the School of Magistracy and in Barristers' Chambers" (Anyangwe, 1989: 197). The Kenyan position slightly differs: university to law school to chambers (Ojwang and Salter, 1989: 88-89). The English-speaking students in Cameroon generally seem to be better prepared for law practice than their French-speaking colleagues, not only because of their pre-university differing education (that the Biya neo-colonial regime is bent on completely assimilating). Even at the then unique UNIYAO's Law and Economics Faculty where both cultural candidates study for the LL.B. degree (better called *Licence en Droit*), their respective workloads reveal a significant difference. The three Law Departments were/are *Droit Privé Anglophone*

(DPA), *Droit Privé Francophone* (DPF), and *Droit Public* (DPU). The Economics section of the Faculty also had two main departments: Micro- and Macro-Economics. A typical workload per week (lectures and tutorials) for the three law departments is shown in Table 1.

Table 1: Workloads of Law Departments of the Faculty of Law & Economics of University of Yaoundé				
Department	First Year	Second Year	Third Year	Total
DPA	19 hours	26 hours	26 hours	71 hours
DPF	19 hours	23 hours	24 hours	66 hours
DPU	19 hours	27 hours	26 hours	72 hours

Executive summary of the detailed discussion of the various courses and their weekly number of hours

Source: Anyangwe (1989: 201-203)

In the first year of study, the law student belongs to no section and only chooses one of these options on being able to successfully pass (through what a legal education

91

critic has appositely called the "great deal of winnowing [that] takes place from year to year" (Anyangwe, 1989: 200)) to the second year. The tradition was/is that most, if not all, Anglophones proceed(ed) to the first option, Francophones to the second. The third option (with only very few daring Anglophones) could be regarded as 'no-man's land'. This compartmentalization only indicates where the core of the student's legal education lies; and not that there is no interaction thereafter. An Anglophone of the DPA department, for instance, still has to take courses such as *droit des obligations* and *droit civil* (which may be core subjects to the counterpart in the DPF department) but only as sub-courses – in the sense that the coefficients are lower in this case than they are to those taking them as core subjects. It is the same with the other DPF counterpart taking subjects like law of contract and family law.

There are courses such as equity, *régimes fonciers camerounais, sociologie générale, histoire des institutions, initiation à l'économie,* and *droit administratif* (this last one being core to the publicists – from the DPU department) that are simply called *matière de tirage au sort* to the *privitistes* of both tongues. According to Dr Fossungu's report on multiculturalism, these *tirage* subjects are concept that Anglophones would meet for the first time only in the UNIYAO. As the name implies, the students are required to study all those subjects. But they will be tested on only the one that is picked at random from the pack on the day of the examination (some critics call it *tumbu-tumbu* examination). The remaining two (there are usually three *tirage* courses per year of study) are then met at the oral examination by those who can make the minimum passing mark (*moyen général*) in the overall written part (Fossungu, 2013a: 107). Dr Carlson Anyangwe, a long-time UNIYAO lecturer, has been quoted by Dr Fossungu (ibid) as describing this *tumbu-tumbu* examination as "examination by ambush", concluding that "No one has been able to explain convincingly the rationale of a system as capricious as this one." Neither has anyone also explained the caprice behind the bar entrance and training themselves.

Some of the Bar entrance irregularities have been exposed by Totale (1996). Anyangwe (1989: 215-216) has also advanced very compelling reasons why the "demonstrably unsatisfactory" present system, whereby aspiring advocates receive their professional training in the chambers of individual advocates – a "system with so many faults" that "can never produce effective and high quality advocates" – must be "scrapped". Some other specialists think that the need for a Law School in Cameroon is urgent. Arguing forcefully that "[t]his country needs a law school in order to boast of a legal awareness, refined lawyers and processed magistrates," Ngwafor (1998: 4) has concluded that "the only solution to arrest the attention of any scholar is the creation of a law school in this beloved Cameroon." Aldarin Ngwafor could scarcely be far from the point as the frustration of Africa's "leaders of tomorrow" by the law school absence can be easily realized from a letter sent to this writer by one of his former UNIBU students. In her letter of June 18, 1997 to writer, Edith Rosa Khumbah Nkokwo wrote in the 3rd paragraph as follows:

> I tried getting into the Nigerian law school without success. The problem is that the University of Buea has not been officially accredited to the law school. Buea has not officially applied; and even if they do, they'll still have problems because the [Nigerian] law school expectations are far more than what we have. They expect in a [Law] Faculty at least 10 permanent lecturers, each with an office, a law library, etc which we don't have. So I have given up the idea of going to law school at least for now.

It should be added that there is even no law faculty in said Anglo-Saxon UNIBU, with the Department of Law there being just a department of the awkward Faculty of Social and Management Sciences. The observations of two researchers on the Kenyan experience can still go a long way to allay these critiques and suggestions. Having discussed pupilage in that East African country, Ojwang and Salter (1989: 89) came to the conclusion that "the making of the Kenyan advocate takes a broad-based and intellectually-focused training at university, as well as technique-oriented training at the Kenya School of Law and during pupilage. Perhaps it may be assumed that such an advocate, subject to his own personal limitations, has been so prepared as to be able to apply himself to the normal work of the advocate." I will 'make bold' (in the manner of Nollywood actors like Kenneth Okonkwo) by going twenty steps further and adding that judges and magistrates be selected from practising lawyers and university professors who have distinguished themselves in the trade and that ENAM, if it has to stay on at all, be a professional school only for civil administrators: knowing too well that this colonial-mentality institution wouldn't even be needed if there is effective local government in this country since efficient and patriotic national administrators would then be better selected from those who have already proven their skills at other levels. There is a lot of support for this theory since, according to a human rights activist:

[o]ne can even see this from the fact that most American presidents have been state governors prior to becoming Number one American. It is, of course, only so obvious that one cannot understand the

national political scene without a sound knowledge about its workings at the local level. Does this thesis not also largely explain the mess we have in Cameroon where *chefs d'état* have always been 'appointed' from nowhere? How can they properly 'manage' Cameroon when they have never even been able to correctly 'manage' a small quarter in their village or place of residence? That has to simply stop, if this country hopes to be well governed (Fossungu, 2013b: 211).

There is thus no Law School in Cameroon; there is only ENAM for magistrates and all other administrators although the training received in some of those 'professional' schools (as well as the universities) leaves much to be desired for effective local government or federalism – sine qua non for the effective education and welfare of "the future leaders of tomorrow" (children). As Professor Peter Bringer and others have shown, the knowledge of their social rank is all the indoctrination Cameroon's civil servants, including judges and magistrates, are given as training in ENAM (Bringer, 1981: 11), a colonial institution whose only-civil-law "entire curriculum was posited on the assumption that civil servants should unquestionably carry out government policy" (Bjornson, 1991: 113). No doubt then that the colonial philosophy of *le patron n'a jamais tort* is currently so unflinchingly embraced in Cameroon.

The boss is always right, they are saying. That is clearly the shooting of one's own foot that a media critic has duly talked about above; being a thing that was inaugurated in 1961 in Foumban by so-called intellectuals in politics through the nonsense they call a Federal Constitution.

ON THE FACILITIES FOR JUDGES', MAGISTRATES' AND TEACHERS' CONTINUING EDUCATION

Yet, people have gone to every length to pass on the contrary. All this continues because of the escapist attitude of the legal profession and academy that would marry well with the absence of law reporting and academic journals as exposed by Fossungu (1998d). Anyangwe is quoted by Fossungu (2013a: 55) for saying that "[a]t the moment there is no consistent and efficient law reporting in Cameroon. There is no official policy concerning law reporting. There is no law reporting council. It is clear that in a situation like this each Court remains in cloistered ignorance of decisions of other Courts. In these circumstances even a loose system of judicial precedent cannot properly operate." Law reports and journals are facilities that enormously contribute to good justiceships. The judge's merit and ability to fulfil his or her duties of dispensing justice, according to Chief

Justice Brian Dickson of Canada, must not be limited to the selection stage but must extend to the entire period on the bench. It has to be "a matter of continuing concern throughout a judge's career. A judge must have the facilities and opportunity to keep his or her knowledge of the law up to date, and to be aware of the commentary and not infrequent criticisms or suggestions offered by legal scholars. This is especially true as we enter the uncharted waters of the *Charter*" (Dickson, 1985: 16).

On the contrary, the glaring judicial inefficiency in Cameroon is compounded not only by the lack of support from the strife-ridden profession and escapist academia. Compounding the dilapidating effects of "*les préjugés des magistrats*" (Laski, 1950: 352-57) will also be the non-existence of judicial contacts. It has been sadly discovered "that no programme exists [in Cameroon] for... [cross-cultural judicial] exchanges. What is even more, the young legal practitioner at the School of Magistracy gets his practical training and forensic experience in Anglophone Cameroon if he is Anglophone and in Francophone Cameroon if he is Francophone. This has only gone to reinforce deep-rooted parochialism and prejudices" (Anyangwe, 1989: 5). To say that there are numerous occasions for judges in Canada (e.g., judges conferences) for judges' continuing training and education is only to state the obvious. Their staggering absence in Cameroon therefore explains why, at its best (in the beautiful expression of some specialists like Professor Wade) the Supreme Court of Cameroon is 'a frail adjudicating mechanism at the mercy of the government of the day.' It is supreme only in the matter of *renvoi* (from the French verb "renvoyer") which simply means "sending back" the case to the Court of Appeal. It is not clear how federalism could have been possible in such a system.

CLOSING REMARKS

It has been shown in the chapter that the entire recruitment and training scheme does not help in the matter of both personal and institutional integrity of both teachers and judges and magistrates; being solely aimed at maintaining and perpetuating judicial dependence and the flagrant administration of injustice. There is obviously much that can be emulated by Cameroonians, in regard of securing judicial independence, from modern Canada. But this suggestion only causes panic in Cameroon. As a Canadian researcher has put it, few people will actually wonder why Third World governments always shrink from, or panic at, the mere mention of "judicial independence." To him, this usually happens only because such governments always see judicial independence simply as a threat to their rights in favour of the people's liberties and rights: which is, of course, true to the extent that these governments always arrogate to themselves "rights" that are properly not theirs. "Judicial independence", he affirms, "need not necessarily be viewed in the negative way (African administrations generally see it) in a society that is truly worthy of the description 'open' or 'democratic'" (Fossungu, 2013b: 142). To substantiate his point, Fossungu quotes Queen Victoria as having declared that "[t]he independence and learning of the judges supported by the integrity of other members of the profession of the law are the chief security for the rights of the Crown and the liberties of the people," before going on to explain that "these words aptly apply to Canada, without modification; but to apply them to Cameroon, as well as the United States, one must substitute 'country' for 'Crown'" (ibid). That is what happens in a society worthy of the description "open" or "democratic", one clothed with a "government under law" which, consequently, leaves the Road to Justice wide open and not closed. *Freedom under Law* (Denning, 1949) is certainly The Royal Road to Justice and vice versa. This also defines good laws.

Third World governments must learn this vital lesson of judicial independence if they really want to achieve even an inch of the progress that they are unnecessarily claiming to be after. Judicial independence is not enough when just stated vaguely in the Constitution. Much more than that is required. According to S.A. de Smith, judicial independence in Canada, like in the United Kingdom and in Australia, "rests not on formal constitutional guarantees and prohibitions but on an admixture of statutory and common-law rules, constitutional conventions and parliamentary practice, fortified by professional tradition and public opinion" (Russell (1987: 75). One can collectively term these elements the constituents of Canada's legal culture. The rigorous resetting of Cameroon's 'Politics without Politics' that is punctuated by the 'Political Culture of Unfettered Appointments' (Fossungu, 2013b: 207-218) to normal acceptable politics ruled by constitutionalism is strongly necessary and called for. Brief, it is a loud call for what some experts like Harold Laski categorize as "*La nécessité d'une réforme judiciaire*" in Cameroon (see Fombad, 2014; and Anyangwe, 1987: chapter 17). The next chapter studies some constitutional fundamentals required for advancing human rights guarantees and respect in governance.

CHAPTER 3

HUMAN RIGHTS, CONSTITUTIONALISM AND THE JUDICIARY IN CONTEMPORARY GOVERNANCE: *ABOLISHING LONG-DISTANCE GOVERNANCE IN AFRICA*

This chapter examines the marriage between federalism, the independent judiciary and justice administration in Cameroon and Africa at large; detailing out some constitutional fundamentals such as balance and supremacy of a community's constitution; aspects that guarantee legality and rule of law. It is the all-time presence of an independent judiciary (which is one of the essential and unique institutions that would help federalism achieve its mission) that makes quite meaningful and understandable all the "debates about federalism and its handmaiden, constitutional law" (Turpel, 1991: 506). This fact seems to be so elementary that even the English Constitutional Lawyer, Albert Venn Dicey (said to be 'famous for his affection for and exposition of the British unitary constitutional system' (Enonchong, 1967: 228)) could not help being impeccably candid about it. "That a federal system again can flourish only among communities imbued with a legal spirit," Dicey asserted, "is as certain as can be any conclusion of political speculation. Federalism substitutes litigation, and none but a law-abiding people will be inclined to regard the decision of a suit as equivalent to the enactment of law. The main reason why the United States has carried out the Federal system with unequalled success is that the people of the Union are more thoroughly imbued with legal ideas than any other existing nation" (ibid: 229). This theory is also fortified by several experts, including Bork (1990), Katz (1991), Holland (1989), and Tocqueville (1945: chapter 6: 'Judicial Power in the United States, and Its Influence on Political Society'). The issue then is: Why are Cameroonians not thoroughly imbued with legal ideas that are required for carrying out (democracy and) the federal system? The previous chapters have provided some answers but we would go in search of further responses in the two main parts of this chapter that revolves around constitutionalism. The first addresses (amongst others) the question of judicial and constitutional rhetoric, showing that federalism is not the only source of litigation; while the second elaborately defines the balanced supreme (federal) Constitution.

WITH SEPARATION OF POWERS, NOT ONLY FEDERALISM PUSHES FOR LITIGATION

Federalism + independent judiciary = veritable development. This is what I would like to refer to as the holy development link or equation (especially for polyethnic polities). Any contrary equation, it would appear, can inevitably only result in the impeccable but shallow rhetoric of community development. This impeccably petty rhetoric will always readily equate any engendered complexity to a threat to "national unity": with no independent agency to say who is wrong and/or right. Cameroon's worsening human rights record is enough evidence of the fact that there was never any federalism there, let alone any marriage between federalism and the independent judiciary. Without this essential union, there is no use talking of the existence of any federation or constitutionalism. The core elements of constitutionalism, according Professor Fombad (2014: 416), can be listed as follows: (i) the recognition and protection of fundamental rights and freedoms; (ii) the separation of powers; (iii) an independent judiciary; (iv) the review of the constitutionality of laws; (v) the control of the amendment of the constitution; and (vi) institutions supporting constitutional democracy and accountability.

In addition to the legal profession and training or legal culture, one can here simply highlight some five legal sources that Canada's Chief Justice Brian Dickson has identified as combining to provide a strong foundation of judicial independence and separation of powers in Canada. These five sources are: (1) the preamble of the *Constitution Act, 1867* (hereinafter *B.N.A. Act*). – the same preamble that the Cameroon legal profession and academy would fearfully join Mr. President in Cameroon in saying is of no constitutional value; (2) Section 129 of the Constitution (which effectively preserved the bicultural nature of the country; (3) Section 96 or the Judicature sections generally; (4) the federal nature of the country; and (5) the *Charter of Rights and Freedoms*, especially its Sections 24, 52 and 11(d) (Dickson, 1985: 6-7). The last mentioned provision of the Canadian Charter particularly stresses the presumption of a charged person's innocence until proven guilty according to law in a fair and public hearing by "an independent and impartial tribunal." Thus, in *Re Charles Currie v The Nicaraguan Escapement Commission* (1984) 46 O.R. (2d) 484, Justice Ewaschuk of the Ontario High Court held that an accused is deprived of this right when tried by a justice of the peace, as these justices at the time did not have the independence required by the Constitution. The status of these justices of the peace before the *Currie* case is seen reflected in the write-up of Shoalts (1991). Further important cases on this Section 11(d), include *Reference re Justice of the Peace Act and R v Currie* (1984) 48 O.R. (2d) 609; *Valente v R* [1985] 2 S.C.R. 673; and *The Queen v Beauregard* [1986] 2 S.C.R. 56.

Some experts on the judiciary have not failed to see in the foregoing *Charter* cases the laudable strategy "of members of the [Canadian] judiciary turning to their own arena to obtain improvements in their conditions of office which they had not been able to obtain by making representations to the government" (Russell, 1987: 160). In short, there is now "such a powerful tradition [of judicial independence] in the United Kingdom and Canada that there may be little point in a fine analysis of the language of the provisions by which it is formally guaranteed" (Hogg, 1996: 161). It may be of interest to see Sections 96-100 of the *B.N.A. Act* which deal extensively with the federal government's appointment, tenure and removal of superior-court judges, subject to the limitations contained in these same sections themselves; as well as and the *Judges Act* s.32 (5) (added by R.S.C. 1970, c-J-I (2nd Supp). and the numerous additions to it. It is here advised that it is more than time enough for Cameroonians to look Canada's way in order to learn how to properly integrate Cameroonians rather than continue to antagonize (some of) them. The most significant areas of such antagonism are in relation to the two legal systems or legal dualism and to language policy or bilingualism – all this occurring because of the absence of an independent judiciary since Foumban where a federation was supposedly created.

That the necessity of the marriage (between federalism and the independent judiciary) being talked about here cannot be lightly contested, is buttressed by a certain book edited by Professor Edmond Orban that "contains contributions from prestigious American, Canadian and European authors who, under his guidance, have studied the relationship between federalism and Supreme Courts in their various societies and within the framework of the European Union."[3] The *Courts* in question can clearly not be *supreme* until they are independent; and there is no such marriage until they are independent. Judicial review (which is simply unknown in Cameroon – Enonchong, 1967: 227-35 & 32-41 however says otherwise) is the most important and continuing relationship that a court can have with other political institutions (see Waltman, 1989: 5; Russell, 1987: 90, 93 & 335). A more detailed examination of this

---

[3] My translation of this original text : "*réunit des contributions d'auteurs prestigieux américains, canadiens et européens – qui, sous sa responsabilité, ont étudié le thème des relations entre le fédéralisme et les Cours suprêmes dans leurs différents pays ainsi que dans le cadre de la Communauté européenne*" (Favoreau. 1991 : 5).

power of review around the world is offered by Cappelletti (1971); Delpérée (1991), Bernhart (1994), and Sonobe (1994). The power of review has thus been said to"constitute an eloquent recognition of the courts as the pivot on which the constitutional machinery of the nation must turn" (Enonchong, 1967: 227). It is only axiomatic that this power of review be one side of the coin of which judicial independence is the other. This part of the chapter continues under two heads. The first examines separation of powers and constitutional democracy, while the second seeks to discover if the argument against judicial politics is really against judicial review or judicial independence.

SEPARATION OF POWERS AND CONSTITUTIONAL DEMOCRACY

According to former United Nations Secretary-General Kofi Annan, separation of powers facilitates the rule of law, which he defined in 2004 as "a principle of governance in which all persons, institutions and entities, public and private, including the state itself, are accountable to laws that are publicly promulgated, equally enforced and independently adjudicated, and which are consistent with international human rights norms and standards" (Fombad, 2014: 417). Rule of law is therefore inconceivable without free courts. Some experts have already furnished a lengthy analysis of the general arrangements of a federation and the connection between its constitution, its courts and its other laws (see Wheare, 1963: chapter 4). An expert on the Cameroonian judicial system has provided a detailed discussion of the composition, organization and jurisdiction of Cameroon's (individual) court(s) from the so-called federal epoch to the present unitary system of government (see Anyangwe, 1987: 127-99). Free courts are a condition sine qua non for the attainment and smooth functioning of any veritable federation or an effectively decentralized polity. It is very significant that, even in unitary 'one and indivisible' France, it is well known that the study of the sacred relationship between Supreme Courts and democracy is not of importance only to federal states but as well to decentralized unitary states. Thus, wrote a European expert called Louis Favoreau in 1991, 'the description and analysis of the relationship between Supreme Courts and democracy is not of interest to just federal states but as well to unitary countries like France because, with administrative decentralization, there is bound to be disputes between the centre and the regions over a lot of administrative issues.' [4] Favoreau`s

---

[4] *"La description et l'analyse de ce phénomène [of Supreme Courts and democracy] présentent un grand intérêt non seulement pour les Etats fédéraux ou quasi-fédéraux mais même pour ceux qui, comme la France, ont une structure*

theorization on France is heavily supported by Schmidt (1990) and Keating 1986). The *grand intérêt* Favoreau talked about has become even grander now with the reality of the European Union, an important part of which France is. It is in a veritable federation that there can be any valid talk of governance of a diverse society (like the European Union) with proper regard for justice, equality and liberty: with the state's integrity being safeguarded at the same time. Imagine a unitary European Union and you must have resurrected Kwame Nkrumah and Patrice Lumumba, with Biya's Cameroon playing impossible possibility. What else should be expected from a country that can actually double the unknown and get the known unknown?

The independent judiciary is normally an institution that should exist to make both decentralization and federalism possible and meaningful. This organ can thus not be limited to federations because it is still central to any democracy *proper* – federal or not. For example, despite its continuing jurisdictional limitations, especially regarding fundamental rights, the Belgian Court of Arbitration has been active in the area of federal-regional spheres of competence. Indeed, as the

---

unitaire, car dès lors qu'existe une décentralisation administrative assez poussée, apparaissent les problèmes d'équilibre entre l'Etat et les collectivités composantes." Favoreau (1991 : 5), citing Louis Favoreu, "Décentralisation et Constitution" (1982) *R.D.P.* 1259.

experts indicate, even before acquiring explicit powers, this Court of Arbitration exercised a tentative and indirect control under the guise of a broad conception of adjudicating federal conflicts. In this respect, the experts have thus concluded, the Belgian "Court of Arbitration seems to share the preoccupations of its German and Italian counterparts. The possibility thus exists for judicial activism... [meaning that] the Court potentially has power to be a serious force indeed in the new political structure" (Shapiro, 1995: 69). Cheli and Donatti (1994) have ably discussed the mentioned Italian counterpart.

The Supreme Court of Canada, on its part, has for over a century decided constitutional cases concerning the distribution of powers between the federal and provincial governments; although it really became supreme *proprement dire* only with the 1949 abolition of appeals to the Judicial Committee of the Privy Council. Until then, appeal to Canadian cases could still lie somewhere else (see Baar, 1989: 53; Russell, 1987: 337). That is clearly not to say though that the Canadian Supreme Court was not then independent. Its independence has long been guaranteed. In the Canadian legal system which is built on a British common law heritage, with the exception of Quebec (which is effectively governed by civil law on matters within its jurisdiction), the judiciary plays an important role in the development and maintenance of democratic institutions in the country. Thus, Beaudoin (1991: 113-118) has lengthily discussed 'Le Rôle Irremplaçable de la Cour'. In other words, federalism (important as it is) is not the only source of administrative and/or constitutional litigation in Canada.

The point to stress is that the independent judiciary (or judicial independence) and federalism have so far found no acceptable places and application in Cameroon; a country which, normally, should be a state in which these issues would be expected to be forcefully instituted and religiously defended. This book largely accords responsibility for the non-existence of these democratic instruments or institutions to the 'bellytics' of ignorant democrats (who are claiming to be politicians) and to the troubling escapism of the legal profession and academia. Without these members of society propping up the existence of judicial independence, even the federalism and multiculturalism that most of them are hypocritically "recommending" for Cameroon would remain ambiguous and confusing. It is then not also surprising why there is a booming deficiency of litigation in the midst of the burgeoning human rights abuses. Added to the previously seen factors responsible, is the constitution itself that not only inhibits any veritable constitutional litigation but also grossly ignores citizen rights and freedoms. As a constitutional specialist has noted, "one cannot escape the rather pessimistic view that an authoritarian resurgence which combines intransigence with strategic adaptability is in progress. Constitutional developments on the continent have reached a point where we must go beyond the conventional Afropessimism or Afro-optimism into Afro-realism" (Fombad, 2014: 447). And these experts could hardly be wrong. In talking about the Maastricht and Brussels projects in Europe, Woollacott held that "the Norwegian decision is, like the Danish vote of Maastricht, a reminder that people in Europe cannot and should not be taken for granted – that they have wishes and feelings of which the Brussels project does not take proper account" (Shapiro, 1995: 148). That can clearly not be limited to one part of the globe, of course. Human rights are human rights, the place of presence notwithstanding (Fossungu, 2013a: 240). Mbaku (2018) also solidifies the thesis where he lengthily discusses Colonel Ojukwu's reasons for Biafra's attempting to secede from Nigeria.

As Shapiro (1995: 148) has noted after citing Woollacott, the various regions within Europe (like those in Cameroon) are too varied and diverse to attempt to impose upon them a single monolithic structure for participation in European (or Cameroonian) events. The Canadian Supreme Court proved this expert's point with its important decision in *Re Secession of Quebec* [1998] 2 S.C.R. 217 on 19 August 1998 regarding any unilateral break-away from the country. The Canadian Apex Court could only do what it did because it is independent. Independent courts are a condition sine qua non for the functioning of any veritable federation or any multicultural democracy like Canada – a country which furnishes precisely the models Africa rightly deserves from Cameroon. No one is here saying that Canada has no problems of its own. Some of these problems that seem to alienate the western provinces have already been extensively canvassed by the experts; including the deep-seated cultural ones that appear to be pushing Quebec to the limit, as also explored in some treatises that have also shown Cameroon boasting of a democracy it is now capable of exporting to the rest of the world, including Canada. Would Cameroon now have sufficient customers for the *denrée* or rubbish that is nothing but toying with human rights, including those to authentic education that is required for citizens' sound understanding of the important and imperative role of the judiciary?

ARGUING AGAINST JUDICIAL REVIEW OR JUDICIAL INDEPENDENCE?

The role of an independent judiciary in a democracy, despite all the criticisms that might be levied against its unelected officials, cannot be overemphasized. Fossungu (2015c: Chapter 1) has catalogued some of the disagreements. Some experts have even seen the issue of such non-electability of judges as nothing but ideological myth that must confront the reality of an elite recruitment process. For whether elected or not the process in social and political terms is never neutral (Russell, 1987: 107; Baar, 1989: 61; Klots, 1973: 84). As mentioned earlier, there is also controversy regarding the role of this institution itself. Viewing L.B. Boudin's *Government by Judiciary* (1932), there have been protracted arguments for and against "legal" or "dishonest politics" (Mandel, 1989: ix; Wellington, 1982: 501-520), with some critics seeing the Court as being given the contradictory task of safeguarding democracy by denying the will of the majority (Lokan, 1992: 163; Ely, 1986; Dworkin, 1989; Matsuda, 1989; Defeis, 1992). Dimond (1989: 2) thinks the solution could lay in what he terms "provisional legislation" to be itself "subject to revision over time." Some other critics see "The Solution" in "A Principled Approach to Judicial Review" (Beatty,

1994: 15-23) or what some experts call judicial 'pragmactivism' (Bearnett, 1987).

Some other experts, after carefully reviewing the arguments, saw only a central difficulty with most anti-review arguments, firmly positing that such arguments try to prove too much with too little as they argue "not against judicial review, but against an independent judiciary" (Green, 1986: 1040). Whatever the case, by no means should the incessant call for an independent and influential judiciary in this book be equated with advocating for "a government by judges. It [only] means a government by governments, but within a framework of rules, the judges being umpires" (Wade, 1980: 73). Another commentator would seem to have closed up the 'much ado about nothing' in the following thought-provoking words:

> As divisive as the SSM [same-sex marriage] issue is, the United States courts have been able to navigate through it with a lot of carefully thought out rulings that laid down easy to predict paths for subsequent litigation. Litigation in this area, like that on abortion, is heavily charged with questions of morality or religion and no matter the direction of the courts' rulings some of the disputants would always find fault with the process. The question that may be asked

concerns whether those who challenge the court as consisting of unelected officials would still make such claims if the court's ruling went their way (Fossungu, 2015c: 206).

This type of umpiring judiciary, it is strongly argued, is what Cameroonians have, first and foremost, to focus on rather than rushing to create millions of shadows in the name of multipartism, regional and local authorities, etc. Otherwise, it is only confusion because a judiciary can hardly play the umpiring role where these conceptions are actually practised: unless and until it exercises the power of review. It is clear that even constitutional litigation (that is, individual versus state or state organs inter se) is unthinkable in Cameroon because the judiciary depends on the executive for its independence. Yet the chief executive thinks that this independence which is requisite for judicial impartiality has already been granted to the judges through material guarantees (see chapter 4). The judiciary's independence and impartiality are greatly strengthened when there is non-concentration of powers. Non-concentration should not be necessarily equated with decentralization (none of the two exists in Cameroon, hence the current stalemate rocking the country being largely hinged on bijuralism and bilingualism). The current one-manish tendency in

Cameroon is contrary to (1) constitutional supremacy which is also reflected in (2) the amendment formula.

THE TIGER-DNA THEORY: DEFINING A BALANCED SUPREME CONSTITUTION AND SHAMING ESCAPIST SCHOLARSHIP

There is no federation without a balanced Supreme Constitution. As the experts say, it is easy to see how the necessity for a Supreme Constitution in a Federal Government leads to the assertion of the necessity for a written constitution. For where the terms of an agreement are so important, it is natural that it should be thought essential that they be committed to writing. So, while it can be asserted that a written constitution is not logically required by the federal principle, it must be admitted that it is practically necessary (Wheare, 1963: 54, 53, & 55). By a balanced Constitution, the experts refer to one by which no one organ has unlimited power and by which there is legal machinery to prevent violation (Wade, 1980: 77). A balanced Constitution is inconsistent without an independent agency to say or determine when it has been violated and what follow-up remedy or sanction and also to determine what it signifies in case of doubt between the disputing parties

(Bayefsky, 1989: 87). Past errors must be avoided. And to adequately do so means correctly knowing what these errors consist of. The Foumban or Federal Constitution, in its Articles 8, 15, & 47 (to mention just these here), simply clothed the President of Cameroon with powers that are utterly incompatible with democratic governance of any sort. Some of the direct results have been the too many confusing laws and constitutions in this country (see constitutional amendments below) – the inevitable consequences of one-man constitution-making and amendments.

Another way of talking about constitutional supremacy is to find out if controllers are adequately controlled, if controlled at all. Just how and whether these controllers are checked, and whether and how a true balance between citizens and the state is kept are very important matters: they not only distinguish one judiciary from another, but also democratic from totalitarian polities. A society which prides itself with a dependent judiciary, concentration of powers, etc., cannot be democratic; one with an independent judiciary and/or multiplicity of power centres will be. In any polity where the basic rights of citizens are guaranteed from unnecessary governmental interference, the supremacy – not only in the federal sense to be noted shortly – of the Constitution is maintained. Having a balanced

Constitution is thus, not enough until its supremacy over all other laws and regulations can be maintained. The supremacy of a Constitution is simply nonsensical when it is, in the first instance, not balanced. If this supremacy attribute is embedded in the Constitution, coupled with a lively political citizenry, one should have already settled the vexed question of the control of the controllers; controllers who can hardly be so controlled where the Constitution is not supreme. This essential quality of the document (its supremacy) would constitute, as it were, what has been termed the federal principle, a principle which is, itself, keenly reflected in the amendment formula.

The UN Secretary-General is quoted for having pointed out that, as a principle, rule of law "requires, as well, measures to ensure adherence to the principles of supremacy of law, equality before the law, accountability to the law, fairness in the application of the law, separation of powers, participation in decision-making, legal certainty, avoidance of arbitrariness and procedural and legal transparency" (Fombad, 2014: 417). By a Federal Constitution's supremacy (as is also implicit in Cameroon's so-called Solid Edifice Theory – see Fossungu, 2013b: 19-21) I mean that the terms of the agreement establishing the general and regional governments and which do distribute powers between them must be binding upon these general and regional governments (Wheare, 1963: 53). Were that the case in Foumban in 1961 (as claimed by Anglophone elites in Cameroon), then there would have been no need for Dr Anyangwe's Tiger-DNA Theory that follows, since the federal principle is necessarily an appropriate dose or medication for fencing or controlling that DNA.

I submit to you that federation no longer commends itself to us. The freedoms we cherish, seek and desire cannot be achieved in the context of any form of political arrangement or co-existence with French Cameroun as one polity. The untold massive atrocities, injuries, sufferings and political, economic, social and cultural emasculation that French Cameroun has inflicted on us over the past six decades are just too profound, wide, and visible to be swept under the carpet for any form of political cohabitation with that country. The colonial oppressor has shown no remorse or contrition for those atrocities. In fact, he has not even acknowledged these crimes, let alone committed himself to atone for them and to turn over a new leaf. Quite the contrary. He behaves like the repeat psychopathic offender. He laughs and boasts about his crimes, his cunning, his fraud, his treachery, his violence and his duplicity. He is fundamentally evil and untrustworthy. Even in the unlikely event of

France ordering him to commit to something, he cannot be trusted to respect his plighted word or written commitments. A tiger never changes its spots. No amount of rain and detergent can remove those spots because they are part and parcel of the tiger's DNA. We should therefore be wise and not make another monumental mistake, this time an eternally fatal one (Anyangwe, 2017).

All what is theorized in the above passage (and the others like it in chapter 1) would only go to clearly show that there was no federation formed in Foumban at all; also only obliquely (rather than openly) indicating that France is the real coloniser to be ordering, not East Cameroun that they are openly crediting with that status. Failing to straightforwardly call a spade a spade can only give good and very comfortable cover to the unnamed spade. President Ahidjo then, now President Biya, could do and have been doing all of what they are being accused of because there has never been any federation created in Cameroon to imperatively bind their actions and deeds at the national level (if the *tumbu-tumbu* LDGT (aka government by ambush) can even allow that there be any other level at all). The imperative binding on both levels in a federation is a logical necessity from the definition of federal government itself because, if the various governments involved are to be coordinate (as they should be) with each other, neither of them must be in a position to override the terms of the agreement concerning the powers and status which each is to enjoy. Therefore, insofar as the agreement regulates their relations inter se, it must be supreme, if there is to be any federation. This supremacy might however not be very essential with respect to some other "matters of governmental organization which do not bear directly upon the mutual relations and status of the general and regional governments" (Wheare, 1963: 55). Professor Wheare is here alluding to matters of purely specific to local concern, having no bearing on what experts usually refer to as *intergovernmental* relations. That is even precisely why each of the regional governments must have its own laws (and other institutions) to take care of these latter matters specific to itself; not having to call upon the central government to enact one for it, as was the case with West Cameroon whose Constitution came from Yaoundé twenty-four days after 'federation' that had supposedly taken place on 1st October 1961 (see the West Cameroon Constitution of October 25, 1961, titled *A Law to Establish a Constitution for the Federated State of West Cameroon*).

Neither should any of the federating states or provinces have the central or common government dictating to it all the minute details as to how and when to run the region of the country supposedly under its authority. Professor Dr Bernard Nsokika Fonlon, for example, has rather objected to this statement of fact and of principle, claiming (in his discussion with Professor Jacques Benjamin in Yaoundé on 15 September 1969) that 'such dictation is not an innovation of the Foumban Enterprise because it is the same with other federations, notably those of the United States of America, Soviet Union and Switzerland': *"la Fédération camerounaise n'innove pas dans cette domaine; les constitutions américaine, soviétique et suisse notamment contiennent des normes obligatoires applicable aux Etats fédères"* (Benjamin, 1972 : 20). It is, the argument thus goes, not unique to the Cameroon Federation. One doubts not only that the central government in all the cited federations does this dictation, but also the claim of the Foumban Federation's constitutional supremacy. There are many further claims from the country's English-speaking constitutional experts that the Foumban Constitution is supreme "because it constitutes a direct enactment of the sovereign Cameroonian People, assembled through their representatives at the Foumban Assembly" (Enonchong, 1967: 22).

One can really begin to see why some crisebacologists (balanced and objective thinkers) like Dr Fossungu have taken the time off their busy schedules to engage in elaborately "Laughing at the [Cameroonian] Academia" (Fossungu, 2013b: 1-49). It is also clear that some of these intellectuals have forgotten intentionally to see what the clear-sighted would easily see, namely, that "when the relationship between the executive and the other two branches of government [in Cameroon] is reviewed critically, even just on the basis of what the constitutional texts provide for, it becomes clear that these constitutions have done nothing more than pay lip service to the concept of separation of powers" (Fombad, 2014: 435). There is scarcely any iota of supremacy to be found in any of Cameroon's constitutions to date: beginning from, and including, the so-called federal one. Yet, hear the 'intellectuals in politics' further telling the questioning youths that the same "Cameroon [Federal] Constitution confers powers, separates and limits it [sic]. It confers express, implied and inherent executive powers on a Federal President; and express powers on the unicameral legislature called the National Federal Assembly; and the Judiciary [whose] ... independence [is] secured by a Federal Judicial Council" (Enonchong, 1967: 22). Is this wishful thinking or constitutional and legal scholarship? Could some sort of corruption also be involved here?

Dr Fombad`s analysis whose objective "is to see how this decline [in constitutionalism] could be arrested to ensure a return to substantive and effective constitutionalism" (Fombad, 2014: 412) has thus "focus[ed] on five main issues: the recognition and protection of human rights; the attempts to prevent dictatorship through a separation of powers; the strengthening of the rule of law through independent judiciaries; and judicial review and the problem of accountability, especially corruption" (ibid: 430-31). It is an open secret, according to Abiabag (who was writing in 1990 about the techniques of protecting public liberties in Cameroon public law), that in Cameroon "all powers are concentrated in the hands of the POR to the extent that any attempt at checking constitutionality and arbitrariness in administration simply becomes a direct challenge to every action of the POR, both as a private person and as a public official."[5] That is how these Cameroonian constitutional documents and the (English-speaking) experts on them have distorted everything about governance and human rights protection. Protection indeed! And the amazement is more especially so when one considers that only the Francophones appear to correctly grasp the absence of separation of

---

[5] "*le pouvoir est ordonné autour d'un homme, le Chef de l'Etat, qui concentre entre ses mains l'essentiel sinon tous les pouvoirs. Dans ce contexte, le contrôle de la légalité, moyen de limitation de l'arbitraire de l'administration, apparait comme étant un contrôle sur l'action du Chef de l'Etat….*" (cited in Anyangwe, 1996: 821).

powers in Cameroon. All this confusion from the English-speaking intellectuals can by far elucidate why only the change of the useless name (deletion of 'United') effected by the 1984 Constitution has had to occasion all the wild cries from the English-speaking community in Cameroon. In other words, one has to wonder why there was no such outcry in 1972 (with the changing of 'federal' republic to 'united' republic by that year's constitution), absent gross distortion by the 'intellectuals in politics'? The simple fact is that there was no federation created in Foumban as there was no independent judiciary to umpire it. Neither was there even decentralization nor democracy proper – to distinguish from Cameroon's foolish or inverted *démocratie sans débat, donc sans compromise*, punctuated by what some decoders of "Advanced Government" aptly call the *"Rule of Higher Unknown Laws"* (Fossungu, 2013b: 141-46).

Some specialists have already traced the supremacy of the federal constitutions of the United States, Canada, Australia, Switzerland, (former) West Germany, India, the defunct Rhodesia and Nyasaland, Malaya, the West Indies, and Nigeria (Wheare, 1963: 54-55). It is interesting just noting that Cameroon does not figure in the list, meaning clearly that it has never been a federation at any time in its history. Two of the above unions (Canada and Switzerland) are particularly intriguing in this issue of supremacy. At first sight, that of the Swiss appears to be "less assured". But one is cautioned by Professor Wheare not to take this to signify that the Swiss Federal National Assembly possesses a legislative power that is superior to the Constitution. That cannot be the case since that body cannot amend the Constitution, being expected to keep within the Constitution's powers – "although no Court is given power to declare when it transgresses its proper limits" (ibid: 55). Dr Enonchong says Cameroon's Foumban Constitution greatly resembles that of the USA (Enonchong, 1967: 23). But unlike other federal Constitutions "the Cameroon Constitution does not state that it is the supreme law of the land. Does this mean that there is a higher national-law than the Constitution in Cameroon?" (ibid: 21). Dr Enonchong's answer to his own question is that the "preponderance of juristic opinion, together with that of Hans Kelsen..., would seem to indicate that the Cameroon Constitution is by necessary implication a fundamental law from which all other Cameroon municipal laws derive their legal validity" (ibid).

THE SUSPENSION AND TERMINATION OF THE REGIONAL AND LOCAL AUTHORITIES: THE LEGALITY WITH UNSUPREME CONSTITUTIONS?

This contribution strikingly differs with the learned doctor by saying YES. There is actually a *higher law* than the Constitution in Cameroon (and it is high time the idea be chased out to make place for the kind of Constitution that promotes and protects human rights). That *higher law* exists not only by virtue of the absence of express declaration of supremacy in the Constitution. Apart from what other crisebacological commentators like Dr Fossungu have already said about the *Higher Unknown Laws*, the issue can also be specifically demonstrated here legalistically with the suspension and termination of the regional and local authorities. By the 1996 Constitution, the Regional Councils and their Bureaux may be, respectively, dissolved and suspended by the POR. That, alone, can be perfectly normal as we can see from the definition of administrative devolution or decentralization. Decentralization has been defined as the conditional diffusion of specific powers by a central government subject to recall by unilateral decision (Britannica, 2002: 712; Kneier, 1939: 12-15). This is what some experts like Professor Hogg of Osgoode Hall Law School have termed "devolution" in the case of a unitary state with diversified power centres, such as Ottawa and the two Territories of Northwest and Yukon (Hogg, 1996: 101 n.13). The devolving legislation in question, in regard of the two Canadian Territories, are *Northwest Territories Act*, R.S.C. 1985, c..N-27 and *Yukon Act*, R.S.C. 1985, c.Y-2. Nunavut is now the third Canadian Territory. This modality is easily found in what some specialists have described as 'highly decentralized unitary states' in Europe but it is not limited thereto. Even Europe's "highly centralized states" as Britain and France (Shapiro, 1995: 2 n.2) can still have it. The example of the United Kingdom and Northern Ireland, as well as the September 1997 referendum in Scotland for a regional Parliament should also be noted.

An associated problem is that of distinguishing the foregoing model of 'devolution' from 'devolutionary federalism'. The distinction, of course, lies in the prerogative of the central government in the former (administrative devolution) to extend, restrict, or cancel at will the devolved powers to the regions, as can be the case of the UK and Northern Ireland as well as Ottawa and its two (now three) Territories (Hogg, 1996: 98). In this instance, the treatment of these administrative units in law does not differ from that of any other municipal corporation. Municipal Corporation has been defined by C.B. Elliott's *The Principles of the Law of Municipal Corporations* as "a corporation which has received a charter as a device and agency of the state for the accomplishment of work of local government within a designated area, and to that end is entrusted with broad powers of local legislation and administration. It comprises as its members the inhabitants of the area" (Kneier, 1939: 6). This is clearly not the case in devolutionary federalism – there being the doctrine of 'co-ordination' of both levels (see Fossungu, 2013b: chapter 1), a requirement that can only go to enhance the judiciary's independence and activist role. This is a sine qua non for the promotion of democracy and human rights in contemporary politics around the globe. Said globe appears to exclude that part of it called Cameroon. Or, is it really *Come-And-Run* (because of its 'jamais-vu' brutality, as some comedians now say)?

The abnormality in Cameroon's decentralization case has to do with the reasons for the arbitrarily taken actions by the central government (the POR, to be accurate) which are to occur when the regional and/or local organs: (1) carry out activities contrary to *this Constitution*; (2) undermine the security of the State or public law and order; (3) endanger the State's territorial integrity; and (4) are "guilty" of 'other cases to be laid down by law' (1996 Constitution, Articles 59 & 60). A voluminous book can be written on just these four factors and much in their regard is already available in existing books on decentralization and democratic governance. I would thus only discuss the *higher law* issue which turns particularly on the fourth reason that also violates the sacrosanct principle of non-retrospection. How exactly does one know what activities are "contrary to this 1996 Constitution" until one has the *higher law* 'laying' that Constitution down? And until one has that laying-down law, how are Cameroonians (or the Regional Authorities) to be guilty, under this yet-to-be-laid-down Constitution, of those cases still to be provided for? Has the 1996 Preamble (which has now been vainly constitutionalized in Article 45: "The preamble shall be part and parcel of this Constitution") not expressly forbidden "the [higher] law... [from] hav[ing] retrospective effect"? That is the dictate of the 1996 Constitution's Preamble (5th paragraph, 9th principle, 1st sentence). The principle of non-retrospection of laws is also embedded in Section 3 of the CPC.

The general idea of *nullum crimen sine lege, nulla poena sine lege* (no crime without law, no punishment without law) is an important principle of legal and criminological jurisprudence (Silverman and Teevan, 1986: 5-6; Denning, 1980; Cohen, 1977). The main rationale behind the principle is that it is unfair to punish persons who, when they acted, did so in good faith thinking they were not breaking the laws. In addition, individuals will not be able to act rationally because they can never know the legal consequences of their acts, due to the potential of these acts later being declared illegal (Silverman and Teevan, 1986: 6 & 12 n.10). Moreover, the same Cameroonian 1996 Preamble goes on (and this is very important) to ordain that "No person may be judged and punished, except by virtue of a law enacted and published before the offence committed" (1996 Constitution, Preamble, 9th principle: 2nd sentence). This principle of legality, which is also embedded in Section 17 of the CPC, has been discussed by Maneli (1994: 106). This principle of legality is a fundamental rule built into any democratic system of criminal and constitutional justice; and it may seem so elementary that one does not need to mention it, but one must always keep it in mind. The self-evident principle can be described as 'the rule of law' – fairness in the formulation of the definition of criminal offences and the rules that govern the determination of guilt (Parker, 1986: 16).

Now, if by endorsing the 1996 Constitution (which Ofege (1995) theorizes as being completely out the question for the bulk of Cameroonians) those who do so are regarded as having "committed" themselves to the "offence" to be created, then, it is trite that they cannot even be judged and punished since at the time of commission said *law* had not *already* been "enacted and published." This is an interpretation of the current constitution to protect human and institutional rights that only an independent judiciary can fling into the faces of those responsible for the nonsense being called Constitutions in Cameroon. Crisebacologists are inclined then to completely agree with my earlier postulation that: "Just give us an independent and culturally-balanced judiciary that is jammed with persons of integrity (even if they are all from the same ethnic group or family!) and even the current 1996 unitary centralized constitution will become a formidable 'Federal' Constitution in their hands" (Fossungu, 2013b: 79). Thinking in the same line, crisebacologists would venture to say that, with credible and independent judges, even the current constitution of Cameroon would become a formidable *Charter of Rights and Freedoms*, a theme that is further developed in chapter 4. Without this type of judiciary, even the American Constitution transplanted to Cameroon would be just as meaningless as attaching 'federal' to the name of a *'Jacobinisme unitaire'* (thanks to Professor Carlson Anyangwe for the term) that is being called Republic of Cameroon, a country that is jammed with ignorant lawyers and hungry hypocritical teachers. So, the essential question is: would this type of termination, suspension and the like of those camouflaged regional bodies under head (4) then be legal and constitutional?

Do Cameroon's lawyers have any answer? Is there then not a 'higher law' than the constitution in Cameroon? How is this indisputable fact compatible with constitutional supremacy?

EXAMPLES OF SUPREME CONSTITUTIONS AROUND THE GLOBE

In the same way as the Constitution of the USA (in its Article VI (2)), Canada's Constitution, since 1982, is now the supreme law of the country (see *Canadian Charter*, Article 52, as well as the *Manitoba Reference* of 13 June 1985 which is discussed by Dickson, 1985: 9-10). The 1867 Canadian Constitution (which was an act of the United Kingdom Parliament) did not have such declaration of supremacy: the express provision of which some specialists say "is merely declaratory of an existing legal fact" (Enonchong, 1967: 22). This could explain why Professor Wheare and many other constitutional experts have all indicated how its absence in the *B.N.A. Act* alone did not deprive the document of its supremacy in the Dominion (Wheare, 1963: 54). Like the Constitution of Australia, such supremacy was provided in the *Colonial Laws Validity Act*, 1865 (28 & 29 Vict. C.63). An edited book by Hodgins et al (1989) furnishes further explanation of this complex colonial situation. With or without express declaration, the supremacy of the Constitution, as already seen, must necessitate the existence of some agency which is capable of deciding what the Constitution means and, indeed, when it has been infringed. This must also involve that this agency looks into the Constitution itself to make sure it does not contradict accepted norms and values of society – and to fearlessly shame legislators (like Canada's Chief Justice Bora Laski always did) into changing it, if it does. The Constitution itself should be just in the sense that there must be no clauses in it which are inimical to justice and the rule of law.

Such clauses are, however, legion (taking the form of what the experts call 'framed legislation') in what Cameroon does have now as its own constitution(s). It is high time for change in this 'one-manish' tendency in legislating and legalizing oppression. It is time to legalize human rights and justice administration in Cameroon and, by extension, Africa. It has been long overdue. The whole absence of any grain of constitutionalism in Cameroon has been crowned by the brief discussion on the termination and suspension of the so-called Regional and Local Authorities – the claimed local government. In short, it is not just enough that there be a *written* Constitution regulating government for it to be federal. Rather, "I think it is more accurate to say that if a government is to be federal, its Constitution, whether it is unwritten, or partly written and partly unwritten, must be supreme" (Wheare, 1963: 53). Further discussion on the written/unwritten constitution is offered by Enonchong (1967: 86-92). Supremacy and the amending formula are two sides of the same coin; the second portion of this part handles the amendment formula issues.

THE AMENDMENT FORMULAE WAR OF RIGIDITY AND GERMAN UNCOMMON SIMPLICITY

As the experts would make it clear to us, constitutional stability and the certainty and predictability that go with this are important elements of constitutionalism and respect for the rule of law. In fact, as they have concluded, a constitution will lose its value as the supreme law if it is frequently and arbitrarily changed to suit the political convenience of the ruling elites (Fombad, 2014: 425). Yes, this is particularly the case with Cameroon in particular and generally the "Central African region [which] is seriously lagging behind the rest of the continent in progress towards constitutionalism and respect for the rule of law" (ibid: 448). No doubt then that Cheikh-Tidiane Gaye said what he has been cited for saying; namely, that conflicts in

Central Africa were so serious that they were a menace to security and peace in Africa as a whole. Let the amendment tales in then to certify. Amendments to the German Basic Law are governed by its Article 79. The procedure, according some writers, is relatively easy, when compared with the amendment formulae contained in other federal constitutions. By this German Article 79, amendments are secured by a two-thirds majority in each House (Bundestag and Bundesrat), with neither direct Lander participation nor popular consultation. The one notorious disadvantage of this relatively straightforward constitutional reform is that "the courts lose their dimension as constitutional battlegrounds and become more circumspect in their decisions" (Shapiro, 1995: 22). In Cameroon constitutional reform is not straightforward (in the sense of not being known). Yet, the courts do not have, let alone lose, their dimension as constitutional arena. Why? The escapism of the watch-dogs of society, the lawyers in particular, would largely explain it. This attitude is further brought out in the specific discussion of the amendment formulae of a number of federal constitutions, including Cameroon's.

KNOWING THE UNKNOWN STRAIGHTFORWARDNESS WITH STIFF AMENDING EXTREME CONCLUSION?

We has discussed the amending procedures of several federations at pages 55-57 of his celebrated treatise, noting that an obvious corollary of a supreme federal constitution is that the power of amending it in regard of matters affecting relations of both levels must not be confided exclusively to the general or regional governments. Both levels and/or the people have to be concerned in the process (Wheare, 1963: 55). He further notes how the association of the people with the general legislature in the process was borrowed from Switzerland, concluding that the Canadian formula is "an interesting example" because "the requirements of federalism are carried to extreme conclusion" (ibid: 56). A detailed discussion of these Canadian 'extreme requirements' or procedures can be found in the books of Anne Bayefsky (1989) and Bernard Bissonnette (1963). Said extreme conclusion is that no authority in the country (government or electorate) has power to alter the division of powers between the central and regional governments. Such power at the time (it is, of course, different now since the 1982 patriation of the country's constitution) rested solely with the United Kingdom Parliament. The experts have demonstrated the dangers to the Canadian federal union that was involved in the UK Parliament almost always acting in this matter as if it were simply the agent of the Dominion government. This led Canadians to recognize that they had to devise some alternative method – hence patriation (see McWhinney, 1982). Was it similar with the Cameroonian Experience of 1961-72?

It looks like only the Bangwa in Debundschazone of Cameroon can capably answer this query, since they are those well noted for competently 'Knowing and Announcing the Unknown in Africa' just as the Cameroonian POR who can so easily double the unknown size of the Cameroon Supreme Court without much ado. Whatever the case, Cameroonians, as usual, would proudly and irrationally tell liberal-constitutionalists and federalists (Canada, Germany, USA, and others) that they do not as yet have any federal democracies to be so proud of. Cameroon, the argument goes, is far advanced in these issues that it is now willing and ready to export its curious brand to the western states. Negative 'impossibly-possible', thumbs-down Bravo to Cameroon! This book is not going into the fine points regarding this country's ability to do what it is boasting of being capable of doing since some experts have amply taken care of that *denrée* exportation business. The consequence of this inverted and curious pride of Cameroonians is that a lot of the issues in Cameroon have simply left several people, who are normally supposed to show the way, bewildered. Why wouldn't they be until they are well schooled in Four-Eyesism or HISOFE? For example, some critical minds have pointed to the United States Federal Constitution which, between 1663 and 1963 (a period of roughly 300 years), had been amended only twenty-two times. Canada's 1867 *B.N.A. Act* had, until 1962 (that is, in the space of 95 years), received fourteen amendments, among which only two touched on the distribution of powers between the Dominion and the provinces (Wheare, 1963: 56 n.1 & 56, respectively). The Canadian situation is attributed to its Constitution being partially rigid in the sense of requiring some complex procedures to modify it. But even with the German easy formula, 48 years after adoption of the Basic Law they were still at "the 39th Constitutional amendment of June 28, 1993" (Flanz, 1994: v) – with most of these reforms being necessitated by the reunification of the two German states. It should be noted that between the 39th amendment and 22 December 1993, there was only "one more constitutional amendment, dated December 20, 1993 which was published as № 68 on December 22, 1993 in BGB/1 on p.20089" (ibid). Flanz (ibid: vii-x) gives some chronology and updates on German amendments in the 1993-1994 period.

On the other hand, just the marvellous inflation of legislation (and the dearth of ligation as seen above) in Cameroon can tell the whole story of the ease of constitutional amendments and, therefore, absence of constitutional or conventional separation of powers. Indeed, it plainly requires writing a voluminous book within this one to account for a substantial part of all such laws/constitutions and their amendments in Cameroon. Can anyone even be able to catalogue *all* the constitutional amendments in Cameroon since 1961? It is very problematic indeed, if not totally and constitutionally confusing. For example, the 1991 Constitution *revised* that of 1984 which had also *revised* the very controversial one of 1972 that had itself *revised* the *soi-disant* 1961 Federal Constitution. But, strangely enough, the 1996 Constitution, without in the least alluding to the one of 1991 in particular, is still "*portant révision*" but on the already revised 1972 Constitution. Why? The import of all this is either that the two or three or four or five... *révisions* in between are without effect; or, if with effect, that the 1991 (and 1984) Constitution(s) would still apply alongside that of 1996. Which of these alternatives is correct? This issue also stiffly brings to the forefront the age-old difficulty of conclusively determining which of the plethora of laws/decrees in Cameroon is/are actually a new constitution or a mere amendment of an already existing one (see Fossungu, 1998e).

I wonder how Dr Charles Manga Fombad could have navigated the matter to give us the information he furnishes. Did the University of Pretoria law professor take all these imponderables into consideration? In his Table of "Frequency of changing and amending constitutions" (Fombad, 2014: 426), [6] Dr Fombad indicates for "Year of adoption of new Constitution" for Cameroon as follows: 'New Const 1960; New Const 1961; New Const 1972; New Const 1996;' (ibid, semi-colon supplied) and for "Year of amendment of Constitution", he puts in: 'Amendment of Const 1969; Amendment of Const 1975; Amendment of Const 1984; Amendment of Const 2008' (ibid, punctuation supplied). No mention is made of the 1991 Constitution and the professor (a Cameroonian too) fully agrees with Dr Ondoa [7] and others when he also indicates that "[a]lthough what we

---

[6] It must be noted that the professor adopts the information in the Table from other sources. He makes it clear that "This information is compiled from data made available at 'Comparative constitutions project: Chronology' http://comparativeconstitutionsproject.org/chronology/ (accessed 31 August 2014). It has, however, been corrected and updated with information from other sources" (ibid).

[7] As this Francophone public law lecturer at the Université de Yaoundé has put the same point in French, "*[l]a première question que cette loi [de 1996] suscite est formelle. L'on est en droit de se demander, en effet, si le nouveau texte procède d'une simple révision constitutionnelle ou de l'adoption silencieuse d'une nouvelle Constitution*" (Ondoa, 1996 : 12).

refer to here as the Cameroon Constitution of 1996 is officially referred to as 'an amendment to the 1972 Constitution', the reality is that the extensive nature and scope of the changes (replacement of the earlier Constitution which had 39 articles with one that has 69 articles) goes well beyond anything that can be referred to merely as an amendment or revision of the previous Constitution" (Fombad, 2014: 428). And that modification inexplicably completely ignores other amendments to the same 1972 document.

The 1991 (and previous) Constitution(s) cannot now be ignored in any sane constitutional discussion in Cameroon. This is because the so-called new institutions of the Cameroon Republic provided for under the 1996 Constitution have to be set up *progressively* and, while these institutions are being set up and until such time that they are set up, *the existing institutions of the Republic shall remain in place and shall continue to function* (1996 Constitution, Article 67(1) & (2), emphasis added). This book cannot, therefore, consider to be outdated the 1991 Constitution which appears to be the latest solid version of the said existing institutions. Furthermore and much more graphical is the fact that "until such time that they are set up" in the Article 67 in question is endlessly dependent upon the current president's discretion, whims and caprices. Thus, a renowned constitutionalist has told us thus:

> The second issue that should be discussed here is that of non-implementation of constitutions. Many governments, under pressure from both internal and external sources, agreed to changes to their constitutions, which some had no desire to implement. An extreme example of this is the Cameroonian 1996 Constitution. It took more than a decade for most of the new changes that were introduced in that Constitution to be implemented. For example, it provided for decentralisation (articles 55 to 60), only part of which was carried out in 2008, that is 12 years later. The changes from provinces to regions (article 61) only took place in 2012 (14 years later) and the Senate (articles 20 to 24) was finally established in 2013 (15 years later). The Constitutional Council (articles 46 to 52) is yet to be established. For many years, it was uncertain whether it was the 1972 or 1996 Constitution that was in force. The story of non-implementation of constitutional provisions is the same in many other countries in the [Central African] region. This explains why there is often this wide gap between the constitutional text and constitutional reality (Fombad, 2014: 446).

Only the presence of an independent judiciary can close the text-reality gap and the equally graphical fact following, namely, that, even before those projected institutions are set up, the incumbent POR, who shall remain in office until the end of his current term (Article 67(2)(a)), has all the powers in the world (under that same document) to cut and nail another one of these unusual Constitutions that will simply send the present 1996 one to the dustbin before the end of that his current term. This Article 67(2)(a) is just a continuation from the federal document that automatically subordinated Anglophones (through their Prime Minister John Ngu Foncha) to a second class 'until the end of President Amadou Ahidjo's current term of office' as president of the federation (Federal Article 52) As a rule, "current terms" in Cameroon (and most African countries) just never end, particularly because of Article 9 of the 1996 Constitution which states:

(1) The President of the Republic may, where circumstances so warrant, declare by decree a state of emergency which shall confer upon him such special powers as may be provided for by law.

(2) In the event of a serious threat to the nation's territorial integrity or to its existence, its independence or institutions, the President of the Republic may declare a state of siege by decree and

take any measures as he may deem necessary. He shall inform the Nation of his decision by message.

This 1996 Article 9 is the successor to Federal Article 15, a provision which obviously and practically renders Cameroon's glorified federal amendment formula of no consequence (see Fossungu, 2013b: 44-49).

In view of securing constitutionalism and the rule of law, the main reforms that have been suggested by an expert can be summarised into four main points which include:

> [f]irst, the constitutional instability caused by the frequent making, unmaking and remaking of constitutions, whether by revision or recrafting of new constitutions leading to abusive arbitrary changes, can be checked by restricting all constitutional changes to a permanent constitution review commission. This commission should be constituted in such a manner that no political party holds a majority and it should have exclusive powers to review and recommend amendments to the constitution (Fombad, 2014: 447).

The plain fact remains that the changing formula is not even the real issue; it is judicial dependence that is responsible for such nonsensical amendments going through. It is the same absence of an independent judiciary that also properly explains the assimilationist language policy in Cameroon. Some freedom and judicial independence strategies are specially examined in the next and final chapter.

CHAPTER 4

IS INTERNATIONAL HUMAN RIGHTS LAW REGULATING NATIONAL CONSTITUTIONAL JUSTICE IN AFRICA? TOWARD A CHARTER OF RIGHTS AND FREEDOMS IN CAMEROON

Yes, as I have said earlier, Cameroonians can easily have their dream society even with their current 1996 Constitution: Provided that they are ready to firmly stand behind their judiciary which should then be able to competently make the requisite *lecture courageuse* of the document to build up a *Cameroonian Charter of Rights and Freedoms*, one encouraging and promoting genuine multiculturalism and equality in both legal and linguistic cultures and the sexes. The way to successfully defending human rights is collective and non-discriminatory. Since the protection of Cameroonians' rights and freedoms is linked to an independent arbiter, securing judicial independence must become a matter of the involvement of everyone in monitoring violations of not only their rights and freedoms, but also those of neighbours. There is also the pressing necessity for further putting into place by Cameroonians themselves a system of reasonable checks and balances (as already suggested above) which must also be jealously upheld. These are some possible solutions to the existing gross and unsanctioned human rights violations. It is thought that the unsavoury experience of the past fifty-nine years (since the so-called independence in 1960) must surely have taught Cameroonians in particular and Africans generally that no amount of waiting on the president and his 'barons' can ever change things. Contrary to the thinking of some Cameroonian lawyers and opposition members, the simple lesson of politics proves that no one would voluntarily surrender dictatorial powers. Every person would be a dictator if he or she can. Freedom is always seized, never granted; meaning that people who are not prepared to fight (and even die) for their freedom should simply forget about liberty.

Talking of *Charter of Rights and Freedom*, as this chapter's title does, would make it appropriate to emphasize over and over that a *Charter* would be useless without an independent agency to interpret and make it a living document. This is especially so because of "the fact that the sometimes lofty ideals expressed in the constitutions do not reflect or correspond with actual practice and there remains a wide gap between the constitutional text and practice" (Fombad, 2014: 430).

The presence of an independent judiciary would obviously narrow tremendously (if not completely efface) such space. This chapter is strongly advocating for the judicial organ that can do the job and has three parts. The first surveys the contention on the causes of judicial dependence in Cameroon; the second dissects some proposed recommendations for the effective institution of judicial independence; and the third moves toward creating and enforcing a Charter by exposing courts as legislators, inviting Cameroonians to unflinchingly learn to live with the Preamble or the new Charter of Rights and Freedoms by bravely backing the judiciary and its independence, and calling for judicial activism in favour of human rights because it is not a question whether courts legislate but simply that of how they should do so.

DEBATING THE CAUSES OF JUDICIAL DEPENDENCE IN CAMEROON

That the judiciary in Cameroon is not independent cannot be disputed at this stage. It is why it is not free that is in contest. The most important concern for this contribution therefore hinges on what should be done to have this human rights organ freed for it to also liberate Cameroonians from the close to a century of colonial bondage under the tumbu-tumbu LDGT's cover of 'independence'. The Cameroonian authorities (largely responsible for covering up and perpetuating the enslavement) have been ceaselessly telling people that Cameroonian judges' 'spiritual impartiality' (whatever that means) has been granted by 'material guarantees'. According to the 1977 address of the POR to the Cameroon Supreme Court, "the material guarantee of the independence granted to the judicial corps must have as its spiritual counterpart absolute neutrality and objectivity... freely accepted by each of its members. There can be no impartiality in a judge without this neutrality in the independence of his functions" (Anyangwe, 1989: 24, emphasis added). The philosophy or logic lessons in this passage are hard to entirely grasp; but did the POR just intentionally forget the 'e' in 'corps'? The query is apt because an activist Cameroonian priest tells us that:

> A Bayangi proverb goes that 'a man who cannot challenge what is wrong is not better than a corpse'. We are living in times where our political and spiritual shepherds have been found wanting in challenging falsehood, and therefore Cameroon has turned into a graveyard, a cemetery of silence in the face of blatant half-truths, divide-and-rule tactics, flagrant disrespect of human rights, mass abductions and killings. The

National Episcopal Council (NEC) has been silent because it concerns the British Cameroons. Though it is disgraceful, we thank them. We thank them for the powerful memento sent to the world that there are two countries in this country. It reminds us of the evil of silence before evil (Jumban, 2017).

Mentan (2017) has also discussed and shamed this "Peace of the Graveyard in Cameroon". Talking of the evil of silence before evil, a formidable proposition against the misguided use of 'apolitical' to remain unconcerned with happenings in the community has also been advanced by Dr H. Bate Agbor-Baiyee of Akron, Ohio, USA. SOBA is acronym for Sasse [College] Old Boys Association. In March 2017, Agbor-Baiyee interestingly put it very lengthily to SOBA-America as follows:

Why is SOBA-America so quiet in the face of the current escalated violence in the sovereign territory of Southern Cameroons? Any justification of SOBA-America's inaction on the grounds that it is an apolitical entity is teetering on buffoonery because, a) the claim of the English speaking Cameroonians or Southern Cameroons' self-determination/independence is legitimate, b) Sasse College itself, as a prestigious citadel of learning, is a product of a rich heritage of Anglo-Saxon political-historical culture of respect for human-rights and freedoms, c) Some of the past and current fearless crusaders of the liberation struggles of Southern Cameroons are firebrand SOBANS. For example, Agbor Nkongho Felix (one of my 1983 classmate) is currently languishing in jail due to the gangsteric colonial incursions of La République du Cameroun in the autonomous territory of Southern Cameroons. I can go on and on. None of us needs civics lesson on the raison d'être of the strategic localization of the towering edifice now called St. Joseph's College, Sasse at the foot of Mount Fako in 'Gbea'. The visionary and pioneering framework of the Mill Hill Missionaries to plant a school of excellence to develop and transform minds that will in turn transform the world cannot be ignored. The question to ask therefore is what are we doing? Owing to Sasse's strategic mission/vision/ alues coupled with its strategic location at the heartland of the English Speaking/Southern Cameroons territory, her role in shaping thought, developmental and political evolution must not be diminished by our desire to cave into our parochial schemes and interests. The ideas of Sasse College are much bigger than our petite-bourgeoisie and primitive accumulation mindsets where our loyalties and focus are narrowed by the corrupted crumps that we grab from the masters' table, better yet from our association with an illegitimate occupational regime. You see; we, SOBANS of all stripes, must exhibit the obligatory intelligence and courage by calling these things as they are even if our parents or relatives are in cahoots with the oppressor; even if they have colluded and are benefactors of the bellicose colonial annexation processes. Our people are in merciless captivity; they are suffering and dying as we speak. Who are we appeasing? As SOBA-America, it is imperative for us to rise up and make a clear, bold and unapologetic statement about our condemnation of what is going on. To sit silently here like dummies and pretend that nothing is going on is not only reprehensible but it is aggravating. This is contemptible! Before I close here, I like to clear this up because I know someone will bring it up; the fact that we may have francophone members of SOBA America is not a source of contention. Rather, it is an advantage to the Southern Cameroons' freedom movement. As civilized people, they (our francophone brothers) should empathize and fully support the movement to guarantee complete and total human rights, dignity and self-determination of their English speaking Cameroonian counterparts, who first showed them (strangers) kindness and hospitality by inviting them in (cited in Fossungu, 2018b 47-48 n.20).[8]

All that can only point to the fact than *granted* independence is practically no independence; also strongly making the case for the urgent need for Cameroonians themselves to fashion the rules in the manner amply suggested by Professor John Mukum Mbaku (2018), for instance, so as to put an everlasting end to what has been castigated as 'tokenistic constitutionalism', as well as terminate the infamous pilgrimages to the 'super-market' Ministry of Finance by their judges. Shouldn't these judicial officials' salaries, for instance, be from a special fund voted by parliament and under the charge of a separate and independent head of that institution (an effective Chief Justice)? Cameroonian judges' salaries are not only not under their control but are also "far from commensurate with the[ir]

---

[8] "If situations were still as they used to be (by bishops not being able to be taken to court in the face of a pernicious silence demonstrated by their brother bishops), I would not hold my pen to write you and I would not have the heart to write this letter to so high an authority as you. Your public silence on the matter of the Bishops of our Church Province being taken to court has provoked this letter from a priest of the Church you belong to. We are not unmindful of the history of La République du Cameroun when it concerns bishops betraying bishops. In fact, if those ignorant of history are doomed to repeat it, the Christian who is ignorant of what role the Cameroon Church has played in the governing of Cameroon is even less fortunate. And the metaphor of Bishop Albert Ndongmo's life is the one great example" (Jumbam, 2017).

responsibilities... and far lower than comparable positions" (Anyangwe, 1989: xi). Is the whole idea behind it, of course, not to facilitate their *selling* of injustice for justice? Moreover, the Cameroonian judge must, like every other civil servant, make the normal "pilgrimage to Yaoundé Ministry to iron out things the way he best can in its regard" (ibid: 38-39). In short, Cameroonian judges' situation is worse than the 'appalling situation' of the Canadian Court before 1882, as ably described by Snell and Vaughan and as discussed by Russell (1987: 137).

The Cameroonian authorities do not see all these remuneration and working-condition issues as the cause of judicial dependence. According to the POR then, it is not the executive branch that is responsible for the pathetic state of affairs. The POR has rather been performing his constitutional duties of 'guarding judicial independence' in Article 37 of the 1996 Constitution exceedingly well. And could he be any more correct in the matter, philosophically speaking? Were the POR wrong in the guarding task, then the judiciary would be perfectly independent in Cameroon. "In Cameroon under our administration", President Amadou Ahidjo told the traumatized Supreme Court judges on 17 November 1977, "it is not the Government that is threatening the independence of the judiciary; rather it is the Government that is protecting it through the status given to the judicial officers, through the vigilance and discipline which my constitutional powers require that I exercise over the functioning of the judicial service" (Anyangwe, 1989: 48). Cameroon's 'Advanced Democracy' just could not be any much more advanced! As an expert on constitutionalism in the Central African region has succinctly put it:

> One of the ways in which the separation of powers and the checks and balances that go with it has been weakened is the excessive powers of interference that the executive, especially the Presidents, have been given over the judiciary. The attempt to separate the judiciary from the other two branches and make it independent in these constitutions is couched in fairly contradictory terms. They contain provisions which usually start by reiterating the independence of the judiciary from the other two branches, but then proceed to state that the President shall guarantee the independence of the judiciary. If the intention was to ensure the independence and, one will assume, equality of the three branches of government, why should it be deemed necessary to entrust one with guaranteeing the independence of the other? (Fombad, 2014: 437) .

A very excellent question from Professor Charles Manga Fombad that sharply cuts through the underlying philosophy of Cameroon's dictatorship that is confusingly but philosophically styled 'advanced [killing of] democracy'! The thesis is coming from one lecturer's 'Lesson in Advanced Government' in which the deconstructing "village Old Man could not but indicate in a playful but meaningful way over his cup of *mbu* or *moluh* that Advanced Democracy (like many other such masterful phrases in the Democracy) was very well chosen; and that it may only properly mean preparing in advance to *kill democracy before it lifts its ugly head in any form*. That is precisely then as far as Cameroonians have out-stepped North Americans [in the democracy business]" (Fossungu, 2013a: 12, emphasis is original). The Cameroonian authorities are never accepting even when they have been stripped naked in public like the Old Man has just done here. And if the POR is doing his job so well and the government is not responsible, and yet all agree that there is no judicial independence: what then is responsible?

The POR again has a ready-made logically confusing answer. "What are threatening the independence of the judiciary are, in fact, the pressures exerted from other sources such as tribal or professional solidarity, social affinities, and complicity with certain interests, which tend to numb consciences and lead to partiality and injustice" (Anyangwe, 1989: 48). Judges in other countries certainly do not socialize, don't belong to professional solidarities, nor have certain interests, to be as independent as they are: Gospel according to St. Advanced-Democrat, with bible in hand called *pleins pouvoirs*. It appears then that there would be no use for President Biya's New Ethnic Group (NEG) as soon as Cameroonians can secure (national and) judicial independence (see Biya, 1986: 27-30). I have ventured to theorize as such because, it seems that weakening the legal profession and academia and destroying poly-ethnicity (through the creation of NEG or *monosity*[9]) are the POR's answers to the problem of the country's (national and) judicial dependence. Yet, and unfathomably so, this same blamed professional *solidarity* must be seen to forcefully exist among judges of the apex court (as seen in chapter 1) so that none of them can interpret the law differently. The graphical issue then is: What must be done to bypass the unintelligible and hypocritical approach of the POR? This question calls for a detailed tackling of some of the issues of this entire book, focusing on how to secure judicial independence for the existence of a Charter of Rights and

---

[9] See Fossungu (2013a: 111-15): discussing "Monosity: Prerequisite for 'Pluralistic Democracy'?"

Freedoms. Following, therefore, is an examination of (1) some proffered recommendations for securing judicial independence before (2) an innovative movement towards a *Charter of Rights and Freedoms* in Cameroon.

STRATEGIES FOR SECURING JUDICIAL INDEPENDENCE

The Centre for the Independence of Judges and Lawyers (CIJL) has made the following proposals as a possible solution to the problem of judicial dependence in Cameroon. "First, the United Nations should establish a mechanism to report on situations in which the independence of the judiciary is being undermined or in which judges and lawyers are under attack. Second, governments should guarantee the independence of the judiciary and the legal profession and prosecute more aggressively those who commit crimes against lawyers. And thirdly, that bar associations everywhere should become more active in the defence of their persecuted colleagues" (Brody, 1990: 3). An un-authored piece in *The Globe and Mail* (Toronto) of 21 October 1991 on page A15 is titled "Lawyers Who Risk Their Lives" and would support the CIJL recommendations. Let's critically examine these proposals, point by point: shortening the three points to (1) the UN option, (2) prosecuting oneself, and (3) selective defence, respectively.

THE UN OPTION: INEFFECTIVE AND PROMOTING THE DEPENDENCY SYNDROME IN AFRICA?

The first point of the CIJL is very plausible, provided effective action can be taken after the United Nations (UN) report. But it is doubtful that this method can bear fruits. "It may be hoped", some human rights experts like Archer and Reay (1966: 22) have indicated, "that in time respect for individual freedom will be protected by formal safeguards, recognized in International Law, enforced in international tribunals, and accepted as binding by the legislative and judicial organs of national governments. But as yet the key to human rights has not been delivered to lawyers." The last sentence may be so in the international sphere only, because lawyers do keep the key in most nations with the effective formal safeguards that are being proposed here. Yorman Dinstein could be right in giving as one of the most dissatisfactory aspects of contemporary international law, its creation of human rights which except within the ambit of regional organizations in Europe and in the American continent, are rarely judged and sanctioned by an international tribunal as against the behaviour of state organs (Dinstein, 1989: 462).

In those excepted areas of the world, "several international tribunals now exist which interpret the various legal instruments. From a trickle in the mid-1950s, as international judges gingerly tiptoed their way into this innovative system of law, this jurisprudence has become a torrent. More than 100 such cases were actually reported in the last year [1989] alone" (Schabas, 1991: v). As laudable as this recent development in international law is, it cannot still make the UN option any better because, as some experts have argued:

> the United Nations (that most Africans continue to look up to) usually is incapacitated by the 'interests-politics' of the gear-lever states of the UN; interests that would often hide behind the 'sovereignty of states' (non-interference) principle; only to quickly invoke 'humanitarian intervention' when that is solely in the invokers' own interests, as many incidents in Africa can clearly show; leading many critics to wonder when Africans would then ever grow up and stop waiting to be spoon-fed by the others – especially when they count so much on the UN that Cassese (1986: 396) says 'now increasingly indulges in the highly questionable practice of begetting ever greater

number of resolutions, as if to conjure up problems and provide for their solution on paper served to settle them in real life' (Fossungu, 2013b: viii-ix).

Richard Dwomoh of Ghana who is currently working with Amnesty International in Norway has also elaborately hammered on the Libyan case which he contrasts vividly with the happenings in Syria (Dwomoh, 2015). Fossungu and Dwomoh are not alone in this business. Some other recent studies on the International Criminal Court (ICC) have found out that there are two questions with multiple answers regarding the relationship between Africa and the ICC. The first, according to **Benson Chinedu Olugbuo** of Nigeria, is whether the ICC is targeting Africa and the second is if politics plays any role in the decision to investigate and prosecute crimes within the jurisdiction of the ICC. For the African Union, the research pursues, the ICC has become a western court targeting weak African countries and ignoring the atrocities committed by big powers including permanent members of the UN Security Council. The accusation by the African Union against the ICC leads to the argument that the ICC is currently politicised (Olugbuo, 2014).

Said targeting by itself should logically be a motivation for Africans to unite and enter the 'big powers' club. Otherwise, what then can be effectively done in this regard by the UN in which "each state, however small, however artificial, has one vote" (Nicholas, 1963: 396)? That remains a matter for speculation in view of the well-entrenched principles of sovereignty, and of equality in inequality, of states (Chen, 1971: 56-57; Fossungu, 1999b: 357-60). And while speculation goes on, what happens to human rights? In addition, the UN (as any other international organization) is made up of so-called advanced states most of whose interests are sort of *protected* by the status quo in the developing states concerned, thus perpetuating (rather than eliminating) the aforementioned *Developer Theory*. The UN cannot thus be understood apart from the interest groups that shape the institution. An institution is not buildings, tables and chairs but those very interests themselves acting collectively for certain specified purposes (Havilland, 1978: 3). This particular CIJL recommendation is thus surely to provide an apt area for the utmost manifestation of what Eugene Sochor (1991) calls 'the conflicting interest of states' and Stephen Segaller (1987) demonstrates as 'double standards'. It could then boil down to prosecuting oneself.

FROM PROSECUTING ONESELF TO SELECTIVE DEFENCE: ENHANCING THE DIVIDE-AND-RULE TACTICS

The second proposal of the CIJL begs the question in so far as the government (this time in the sense of the executive branch particularly) is the very institution which often undermines judicial independence. It is childish (and very Cameroonian) for anyone to expect that the government will effectively prosecute itself. Even in the event of such unlikely prosecution, would it not be both judge and party? Much more evidence of the government not being ready to prosecute itself can even be derived from what some experts castigate as non-implementation of constitutions already seen in chapter 3. It should be note that Justice Nyo'Wakai (one of those that Professor Carlson Anyangwe (1989: xv) describes as 'two of Cameroon's finest judges') has suggested something similar to this second point of the CIJL. Dr Anyangwe's discussion, that 'ablest and finest' judge recommends, of the "place, role, and independence of the judiciary in our governmental system is most illuminating and deserves *serious consideration of those who are in positions to influence policy in this respect*" (Nyo'Wakai, 1989: xix, emphasis added). As to this recommendation specifically, it may be questioned as to who these people 'in position to influence policy in this respect' are. There is only one such person in the present set-up in Cameroon – the POR. Consequently justifying why Fombad has instead suggested the use of independent commissions and that presidential term limits would need to be restored, and the enormous presidential appointment powers should be limited by laying down strict criteria for all appointments and promotions; with this coupling with a constitutional right to expeditious, efficient, lawful, reasonable and procedurally-fair administrative action (Fombad, 2014: 447-48). This is more sensible than the slavish reliance on the current 'one-manish' process since, surprisingly ironical, the New Ethnic Group and other 'crimes against lawyers' are the best means that this *only* person sees fit as means towards guaranteeing judicial (and national) *independence.* To say simply that he should do 'something' 'to influence policy' in that regard is to say that he should influence himself to guarantee that independence: which is just what he *thinks* he is doing; and doing it so well too. This second point has therefore to fall flat to the ground, just as that of *Selective Defence* because the gravamen of this book is even kicking against the fact that human rights defence should be limited to lawyers' persecuted colleagues. That can only aggravate things, as has been stressed in the discussion so far. But it might need reiteration with a critic's postulation in 2016 that:

> Th[e] carried-over critical theory was that the problems in Cameroon are often worsened by the fact that Cameroon's lawyers only talk human rights when their specific interests are in question; not bothering when the rights of other members of society are violated. And that, rather than monitor and defend against the incessant human rights violations by the authorities, some of these lawyers instead go about actually nosing and committing crimes, leading to Maitre Alice Nkom's thesis (in *The Messenger* of 20th May 1996) that the said lawyers 'are running after money like blind men. I am afraid of their future in the profession. They have to go back to school' (Fossungu, 2016).

THE INDEPENDENT JUDICIARY'S QUESTIONS FOR REVIEW IN FAVOUR OF HUMAN RIGHTS: NOT WHETHER BUT HOW

In addition to the specific indication in the foregoing parts of this book, the best answer to the problem, on the whole, lies with the people concerned. The intent is to map out here how they must go about doing this as we move towards an enforceable *Charter of Rights and Freedoms* in Cameroon. The suggestion is that everyone in the country must be actively involved, not just the lawyers, judges, and law teachers – though these should be on top of the list. It is a Cameroonian issue, and not just an Anglophone problem. As already indicated, it is this unintelligent distinction that has been killing human rights defence and protection in the country. It is very important that each and every member of society be involved in the guarantee of judicial independence. Sir Edward Coke, bold and fearless as he was, the Seven Bishops and their Jurors, American Judge Marshall, and others that can be named, should simply have failed in their various judicial independence enterprises if the very people for whom they struggled had not stood by them. In other words, as one criminal law expert put it long ago, "[i]f the American people fail to assume their responsibilities to government, it is not inconceivable that the law could become an instrument of oppression in this nation" (Day, 1964: 12). The public (including members of government as well) must therefore understand that the diminution of judicial independence is the unmistakable preface to the annihilation of their rights and freedoms. Human rights are properly said to be rooted in the collective rather than individual responsibility. And this is only possible with active citizenship and participatory democracy, both of which cannot be divorced from sound civic education. Many legal and constitutional experts have also confirmed that. We thus hear Fombad (2014: 448) theorising that:

> Many of the present constitutions [in the Central African region] contain elements of what is needed to make progress. All that is needed is to stop the threats to undermine some of the important gains that have been made and to keep the pressure to improve on the others. In all this, the ordinary citizens hold the key rather than external forces and actors. With more education and awareness creation, more people will be able to fight for substantive and effective constitutionalism rather than to endure the hardship from the present tokenistic gestures.

A *Charter of Rights and Freedoms* without this basic civic education on the part of the larger public can be of little or no use. A sure 'advanced democratic' reason for the exclusion of political development of citizens in Cameroon? It is thought that if those qualities or characteristics were in place there must by now be a well known and enforceable Charter of Rights and Freedoms in Cameroon. Unlike Canada and the United States, Cameroon currently has no Charter or Bill of Rights and Freedoms as such: despite the confusing desire and call for one that was made about thirty-six years ago (see

Biya, 1986: 41-43); with one such Charter even having been proposed to Cameroon in 1989 (see CBA-CBC Report, 1989). And there is none yet in place? Some people are apt to rush to a 'YES' answer here. But does a Charter under the 'charter' name mean anything if the legal and media professions are not credible enough to see to it that it be enforced to the letter? And do such professionals even need a document with that name (Charter) to be able to safeguard citizens' rights and freedoms embedded in the preamble of the current 1996 Constitution? Perhaps help in accurately answering these questions can be obtained from an examination of the independent judiciary's questions which are necessary for its legislative role, turning on the current Preamble's promises. This task, I must keep emphasizing, can only be done by an independent judiciary.

The institutionalization of inhuman rights and injustice administration that was carried out in Foumban (Cameroon) would need to be radically reversed in Africa through having an independent judiciary. It is thought that only an independent judiciary can very clearly tell Mr. Biya (or anyone else that is Cameroon's president), first, how 'hogwash' his decentralization is: by actually deciding cases such as Bouba Bello's noted in chapter 2. Some Cameroonians continue to think the answer to Eyinga's question in the *Bello* case (as to why the

Supreme Court was not proceeding with the case) is to be found in France; going on to call on that country to 'Democratise Cameroon' simply because 'Fru Ndi Tells France to Advise Biya' (Kfua, 1996; Ndifor, 1996). That is pure daydreaming, especially in view of what has been emphatically delineated above. Those calls were made more than twenty years ago and what has happened till date? To adopt and adapt the words of Mensah-Gbadago (1991), '58 Years of Political Transition: From Ahidjo to Biya and the Hayatou-Yang Connection – How Far Have We Moved?'As an expert has ably theorized in a book on Afrikentication and African Unity, "only Africans can fix Africa for Africans. No one else can do that for them. Africans had therefore better wake up now and take the bull by the horns and let succeeding generations be able to proudly say in their time: 'We had fore-parents who thought of us'" (Fossungu, 2015a: 229-30). Thus, only Cameroonians can free and democratize Cameroon. And they can competently do so in the manner being suggested here. It is thus the securing and guaranteeing of the judiciary's independence that is important.

As this contribution sees it, Cameroon already has a *Charter of Rights and Freedoms* in place. What would be lacking are just credible legal and media professionals and active citizenry to back up the judiciary in upholding and enforcing it. The credibility of the mentioned professionals is of prime importance. A human rights activist seems to have captured the entire dynamics even more fascinatingly when he theorized in 2013 that:

> It has been discovered that a money-chasing legal profession (as is the case in Cameroon) can hardly help in ameliorating things in this country since it cannot properly defend the rights of citizens and businesses, let alone those of other state institutions, notably the judiciary. That could be the main reason why most of the citizens have simply found it more advantageous to simply join the 'voyous club' rather than stand up only not to be counted: since no one is there to defend their defending their rights (Fossungu, 2013b: 147).

The visible activism of the lawyers, journalists and 'men of God' of a society can obviously not fail to embolden its judges and magistrates and, thence, the general public. A priest has captured the case of his own calling so well. I am talking about Reverend Gerald Jumban who has theorized in his un-paginated letter as follows:

> Evidently there is no moral compulsion as pastor to pasture the flock in a particular way. But there is, I believe, a moral obligation as a priest, not to allow oneself be used by tyrants to perpetrate spurious

propagandas against the defenseless. A clergyman, in my definition of that office, would not be someone who takes sides with colonial governors against the oppressed. I strongly believe that a priest worthy of the name should go ahead and dare those forces – morally, non-violently and with determination – that keep millions of constituted people caged in a cruelty so dehumanizing as the yoke over the British Cameroons, our native land. This because, someday history will disclose to him that those who took courage to work for their mother country, those who spoke for the speechless, those who stood for justice, those who listened attentively to the cry of the oppressed, and those who championed the cause for the non-violent restoration of the sovereignty of a nation, have been champions of whom all upcoming epochs will be proud. Your Grace, The cause for the restoration of the sovereignty of the British Cameroons is one built on a big idea supported by legality. You don't kill an idea with the bullet or prison cells. It is established on a winning banner that debate is stronger than the gun. The power of debate and not the debate of power. This power of debate and legality convinces us beyond all doubt that there is a country (Jumban, 2017, altered paragraphing).

It is thus emphasised that the unflinching backing up of the judiciary is what one thinks Cameroonians (from north to south and from east to west) have to be doing rather than asking foolish questions to the judges and kidding themselves that only the unsupported and brutalized judges will be judged by progeny. According to the country's lawyers, "When it will be time for posterity to judge our actions, it will first judge our judges here..." (Fossungu, 2013a: 150). But what are most of these intellectuals of the law now saying, for instance, about the 1996 Constitution's exclusion of political development of citizens in Article 55(2), as has been elaborately critiqued by Fossungu (2013b: 210-19)? Cameroon's intellectuals generally do claim a lot of knowledge and the like (knowledge indeed!); but seasoned observers are simply stupefied to find that they are not even helping the judiciary to ask questions like the following – queries which I humbly think only an independent judiciary (itself inconceivable without the backing of the profession and academia) can ask and give acceptable responses to.

How can "The State... [be able to] provide all its citizens with the conditions necessary for their development" in the 1996 Constitution's Preamble when the same constitution expressly excludes or purports to eliminate their developing politically in Article 55? 'The concerned provision is struck down, therefore, for contravening the Preamble's Article of Faith,' says an independent court. How is this same State to "recognize and protect traditional values that conform to democratic principles, human rights and the law" in that Constitution's Article 1(2) by not promoting the people's political development; and by expressly keeping the Courts proper out of that democracy in Article 4? Isn't the shortcutting of the democratic process involved in this whole arrangement plain enough? How is all this exclusion of the judiciary and the people's political development to tally with the State's affirmed attachment "to the fundamental freedoms enshrined in the Universal Declaration of Human Rights, the Charter of the United Nations and The African Charter on Human and Peoples' Rights, and duly ratified international conventions relating thereto..." (1996 Constitution, Preamble)? Just how on earth will "the State... guarantee all citizens of either sex the rights and freedoms set forth in the Preamble of the Constitution" (ibid: Preamble: 5th paragraph, 25th principle) when the rightful guarantor of the same – the judiciary – cannot exercise state powers and must also be prevented from being independent of potential violators of the same rights and freedoms? What is to happen, for instance, if someone disagrees with the restriction in Article 55(2) and sues to have the excluded political development in accordance with the Preamble and the *African Charter on Human and Peoples' Rights* and others where the right is also adequately covered?

All these queries (and many more) can only drag us once more to the inevitable thesis that Cameroonians Must bravely Learn to Live with Their Preamble. It might be unnecessary now to discuss more elaborately the question of the preamble's validity since the country's authorities themselves have already voluntarily saved us the energy through the same 1996 Constitution by whose Article 65 "The preamble shall be part and parcel of this Constitution." What is even more is that the enthronement of this 1996 Preamble is insurmountably propped up by other sections of the same 1996 Constitution, notably its Article 45 by which duly ratified treaties and international conventions shall override national laws that contravene them. The question now is that of how to effectively turn this 1996 Constitution's Preamble into a *Cameroonian Charter of Rights and Freedoms*. This essential preamble-transformation is all what is important for Cameroonians now. This is because, although the preamble has been *constitutionalized*, the NEG (New Ethnic Group) agenda still seems to stand above the entire 1996 Constitution: until the NEG can be strongly and creatively denied its apparent supremacy using the Preamble's Article of Faith. Cameroonian judges and magistrates and lawyers (as well as the so-called Constitutional Councillors in Articles 46-52 and Senators in Articles 20-24), if they are worth their name at all, must henceforth interpret and review any of the country's 'higher laws' only in the light of this Preamble – Cameroon's own compendious version of a universally agreed *Charter of Rights and Freedoms*.

In introducing the 'Magna Carta to the Canadian Charter' (Schabas, 1991: 1-16), Professor William Schabas of the Université de Québec à Montréal (UQAM) pointed out that, since the proclamation of the *Canadian Charter of Rights and Freedoms* on 17 April 1982, "[t]he protection of the human rights and fundamental freedoms of Canadians from government action and legislation has been substantially enhanced" (ibid: 1). It is well known that "[f]ollowing the proclamation of the *Canadian Charter of Rights and Freedoms* in April 1982, Canadian courts have been enthusiastic and imaginative in the application of international human rights law. [And, as of July 1990, m]ore than 145 post-Charter cases cite international human rights instruments and jurisprudence" (ibid: vi). In fact, the concerned Cameroonian officials and public must note and understand that the power of the preamble is everywhere powerfully asserted. Prominent scholars and jurists have discussed its power and significance, with several authorities being furnished as corroborating its importance for polities that hope to remain viable in the 21st century and beyond. Professor Maneli of City University of New York (CUNY), for example, has demonstrated that "the soul of the Constitution" is freedom. Today, he further states, in addition to the Constitution, we live in an era of the Universal Declaration of Human Rights and other similar undertakings (Maneli, 1994: 103). As Cameroon has ratified most of these undertakings (see Fossungu, 2013b: chapters 3 & 2), therefore, the CUNY professor asserts that "it is appropriate [that] in the interpretation of the [Cameroonian] Constitution: in the event of doubt, one should opt for... liberties and individual rights" (Maneli, 1994: 103). That is why Roscoe Pound and Theodore FT Plucknett would tell us that Chief Justice Coke (who boldly refused to be instructed by the King) "considers the preamble as a key to open the understanding of the Statutes" (ibid: 105). New Jersey's retired 10th Congressional District Congressman, Peter W. Rodino, has put the point even much more forcefully by indicating and stressing that the preamble is both an Article of Faith and a Covenant of Trust so that all other avowed purposes of the Constitution must necessarily dovetail with it in order to be constitutional (Rodino, 1990: 685).

As said earlier, Cameroonian judges and magistrates and lawyers and legislators worth their names must henceforth interpret and review the entire 1996 Constitution and any other laws only in the light of the country's constitutionalized Preamble. To properly do their job in this regard, they must seek to provide correct and appropriate answers to queries like the questions above that have been posed as guidelines (turning on the Preamble's promises). Until all this can be and is done to effectively have an independent arbiter, Cameroonians should stop kidding themselves that they are not running around naked. Because it is only in a country with a proper and balanced constitution (written or unwritten) that "an individual is given a whole congeries of rights, which like a garment surround and protect him" (Maneli, 1994: 103). Wade (1980: 77 & 73) theorizes to the same effect while Williams (1987: 409) also clearly makes "my insistence on the protective distance which rights provide." Hence, "[t]o be specific, the preamble... [must] be resorted to in restraint of the generality of the enacting clause, when it would be inconvenient if not restrained" (Maneli, 1994: 105). The preamble is also important in explaining the enacting clause that is doubtful. Thus, writing six years after

Cameroon's bizarrely 'preambleless' 1961 Federal Constitution, Dr Henry Enonchong (1967) posited that:

> When... a constitutional text presents some ambiguity, when doubts arise as to its meaning and scope, the court does not need to confine itself to an obstinate inquiry into the meaning which, in framing this or that article, the framers of the constitution actually intended many years ago. It must ask itself what would have been their intent if the same article had to be framed by them today (p. 89).

It is simply beyond comprehension why a federal constitution (of all constitutional models) should be devoid of a preamble: except that it could just have been a secret personalized document designed to confuse the general public? Whatever it is or was, the 1996 one has a preamble that the courts and that general public have to now use to bring the confusing drafters to order. They can thus be guided in the exercise (for instance) by Fombad's instructive study that offers a number of measures which "it is argued, need to be taken to make constitutionalism in the region meaningful and effective" (2014: 412). Happily, as previously indicated, the preamble-converting exercise for effective constitutionalism is also sufficiently sustained (perhaps, even to the ignorance of the framers) by other areas of the same Cameroonian

Constitution, especially its Article 45 by which "Duly approved or ratified treaties and international agreements shall, following their publication, *override* national laws..." (emphasis added) It is needless here listing such duly approved or ratified treaties and international agreements that are in place for Cameroon. The preamble in question has itself already done that job by enumerating the most basic of them: some of which have already appeared above in the list of questions for an independent judiciary to ask and provide acceptable answers to. How this type of judiciary must proceed in the matter of overriding laws contravening international human rights norms and practice has already somewhat been largely indicated by Fossungu (2013b: 160-62). What would need to be stressed is that independent judges have the power to draw up a new constitution; that is, legislate when it is necessary to protect human rights.

There is no arguing that courts must, and do, make laws in favour of human rights protection. Professor Laski quotes President Franklin Delano Roosevelt's message to Congress on 8 December 1908 to the effect that judges are necessarily legislators (see Laski, 1950: 152). Judges themselves have unambiguously affirmed it (Dickson, 1985; Diplock, 1964; Deschenes, 1974). The only question then is how (not whether) they do or should do so. Professor Dale Gibson has trenchantly condemned Cameroon, first, for not training its judges in particular in both legal traditions like Canada before, second, concluding that (contrary to the Cameroon unacceptable formula that makes automatons out of judges) there is no denying that courts must, and do, make laws in favour of human rights protection. "Judges trained in both of Canada's major legal traditions know (despite what they may sometimes say) that they are not expected to be automatons. If they did not anticipate playing a creative role, both as agents of justice and as cultivators of the jurisprudential garden, many of our talented lawyers would probably refuse to accept judicial appointments" (Gibson, 1987: 253).

It is known that an activist judge (and every judge must strive to be one) is one who is aware that he or she wields enormous executive and legislative power and that these powers and discretion have to be used militantly for the promotion of constitutional values as well as to protect and preserve the human rights of minorities guaranteed by the Constitution (Baxi, 1987: 172 & 174). Thus, as Madam Justice Wilson held in *Morgentaler, Smoling and Scott v The Queen and Attorney General of Canada*, "the rights guaranteed in the [Canadian] Charter erect around each individual, metaphorically speaking, an invisible fence over which the state will not be allowed to trespass. The role of the court is to map out, piece by piece, the parameters of the fence" (Turpel, 1991: 509). It is useless doubting that only courts with activist judges can perform this mapping-out function. An activist judge's 'faute de mieux executive powers' involve (1) powers of admission; (2) powers of scheduling cases for hearing; (3) powers to form benches or panels; (4) powers of granting 'stay' *pendent lite*; (5) powers of 'suggestive jurisprudence'; (6) powers of scheduling reasoned judgments; and (7) powers of allowing or disallowing a review. And most of these powers may even result in a decision not to proceed to a decision (Baxi, 1987: 169).

This type of judiciary should not be any strange thing, unique to Cameroon that it has to be as awful as Cameroonians have been, and are still being, frightened into thinking. The timeless issues of the 'role of the judiciary', Professor Radhika Coomaraswamy has indicated, have recently been the subject of much discussion in the developing world. The growing awareness of the need for human rights protection, she has suggested, has focused attention squarely on the judiciary, thus making it increasingly impossible for judges to hide behind the doctrine of judicial 'self-restraint' and 'passive' interpretation. This is the more especially because their judgments in the area of fundamental rights are now the subject of growing scrutiny by an international audience. This international audience, according to Coomaraswamy, is now, more than ever before, interested in the need to implement social justice. Consequently, the prestige and legitimacy of the judiciary cannot fail to be constantly called into question as an increasing number of citizens and citizens' groups thrust their numerous grievances directly to the portals of the Supreme Court (Coomaraswamy, 1987: 1). It is certain that judges will greatly fail in their duties here if they allow their hands to be tied by the prohibition against judicial adventurism or activism. It is then truly not a question of whether or not the judges should (and they do) really legislate. Not whether but how, as the experts say; but how in Cameroon?

Of course, the judges must write a better Constitution, as I am here stressing, through their neat and bold construction of whatever law or portion of the 1996 Constitution to protect human rights. They ought then to listen very attentively to Justice Holmes' timeless declaration that "[w]hoever hath absolute authority to interpret any written or spoken law, it is he [or she] who is truly the lawgiver, to all intents and purposes, and not the person who first wrote or spoke them" (ibid: 3). This signifies that the Court's interpretation of the fundamental law of the land must prevail over the expectation of any legislature or executive because constitutions merely express the 'positivization' of higher values and judicial review is the method by which such values are rendered effective (Cappelletti 1971: vii & x; Tocquevill, 1945: 104). Alexander Hamilton, writing in *The Federalist*, made this point exceedingly clear when he said:

> The interpretation of the law is the proper and peculiar province of the courts. A constitution is, in fact, and must be regarded by the judges as a fundamental law. It must therefore belong to them to ascertain its meaning as well as the meaning of any particular act proceeding from the legislative body. If there should happen to be an irreconcilable variance between the two, that which has the superior obligation and validity ought, of course, to be preferred; or in other words the Constitution ought to be preferred to the statute, the intention of the people to the intention of their (legislative) organ (Enonchong, 1967: 228).

Judges must, however, not smile too much and consider themselves sole beneficiaries of these freedom proposals or strategies. These judges, as Brazilian Supreme Court Judge Jose Francisco Rezek instructs us, must only be defended in the common interest of the people, particularly the most humble elements of society and those who most intensely rely on a free, efficient, altruistic, honest and wise system of justice (Brody, 1990: 5). Securing judicial independence is, first and foremost, a matter of the involvement of everyone in monitoring violations of not only his or her rights and freedoms, but also those of neighbours. That is the way to successfully defend human rights, not through the discriminatory or selective method. Second, there is pressing necessity for the further putting into place by the people themselves a system of reasonable checks and balances which they must also jealously uphold. This is what the solution is and their 58-year experience must surely have taught Cameroonians that no amount of waiting on the president and his 'barons' can ever change anything. The simple lesson of politics proves this. No one voluntarily abdicates or surrenders dictatorial power (contrary to what some 'prominent' Cameroonian lawyers and so-called opposition politicians appear to be thinking). Every person will be a dictator if he or she can. Freedom is always seized, never granted. People who are not prepared to fight (and even die) for their freedom should simply forget about independence.

CONCLUSION

Human rights guarantees and protection are the catalysts of development in all its ramifications. A citizen, bold and creative as he or she may be, can hardly exhibit such activism and awareness if he or she is not confident that the courts are strong enough to provide the necessary protection. Those courts can only be strong enough to provide that protection if they are actively backed by the legal profession and academy, and the media (Fossungu, 2013b: 145). Members of these noble societal 'watch-dogging' professions cannot seriously perform this backing-up job if they are unbendingly parochial because this necessarily prevents their being able to accommodate each other's differing perspectives associated with cultural and educational differences in a country like Cameroon. The backing-up function can hardly be shouldered by those who are not daring and imaginative. The colonial philosophy of *le patron n'a jamais tort* that is currently unflinchingly embraced in Cameroon particularly and Africa generally stifles the imagination even more than the 'dogma of parliamentary sovereignty'. Through the type of re-orientation in understanding and perception of the bulk of Africans here suggested, it could be easily possible to formulate "new ways of thinking and acting, new critical approaches to every social, political and juridical institutions, be they [rooted] in the east or in the west [of Cameroon or Africa]" (Maneli, 1994: 1). It is believed that this is not such a very difficult job to do: should the dedication and zeal to be free just be there.

It is my strong belief that a whole lot of things would need to be done by Cameroonians in order to merit the "birds of the feather" description with Canada. They must have to make the required recommended changes and thereby be properly belonging to the Birds-of-the-Feather Club. In other words, Cameroonians must move the gear lever out of the reverse and into an appropriate forward gear; a thing they (like Africans generally) can only successfully do "if political leaders of both language groups are sincere and loyal to national unity and development, bearing in mind that there is no inferior and superior culture in Cameroon."[10] If I were to provide a word-for-word translation of those wise words of Quebec Court of Appeal Justice Bissonnette, I would simply tell readers what it is kicking against – assimilation. Until there is mentality change in this

---

[10] *"si les homes politiques des deux nationalités se coudoient, s'épaulent et tendent, dans une même volonté, par un effort loyal, dans un respect mutuel, affranchis de tous préjugés, persuades selon le mot de John A. Macdonald 'qu'il n'y a au Canada [et au Cameroun] ni race supérieure, ni race inferieure', l'organisme politique sera peut-être sauvegardé et notre nation, vigoureuse, avec tous ses éléments soudés dans un tout harmonieux, pourra, sous l'égide de la Providence, atteindre et réaliser de grandes destinés"* (Bissonnette, 1963 : xv).

African country and the continent at large as here suggested, it is very clear that nothing, absolutely nothing, would have changed if one wrote any constitution that can be written on earth (be it even the American one) and gave to Africans with the egoistic attitude they currently exhibit. Posterity certainly deserves better than that from the intellectuals of Africa, this class being specifically pinpointed because they are people who are thought to be in a better or privileged position to help in getting the continent out of the dungeon.

REFERENCES

Agbor, Avitus (2015) "The Role of the Judiciary in the Promotion of Democracy and Human Rights in Cameroon" 8(1-2) *African Journal of Legal Studies* 145-73.

Albaugh, Ericka A. (2011) "An Autocrat's Toolkit: Adaptation and Manipulation in 'Democratic' Cameroon" 18 *Democratization* 388-414.

Anyangwe, Carlson (2017) "Why Federation No Longer Comments Itself to Us" @ http://cameroonjournal.com/2017/08/02/why-federation-no-longer-commends-itself-to-us-dr-carlson-anyangwe/.

_____ (1996) "Administrative Litigation in Francophone Africa: The Rule of Prior Exhaustion of Internal Remedies" (1996) 8 *Revue Africaine de Droit International et Comparé* 808-26.

_____ (1989) *The Magistracy and the Bar in Cameroon* (Yaoundé: PANAG-CEPER).

_____ (1987) *The Cameroonian Judicial System* (Yaoundé: CEPER).

Archer, Peter and Lord Reay (1966) *Freedom at Stake* (London: The Bodley Head).

Aseh, Andrew (1996) "Finance Ministry Degenerate into a Super Market" *Cameroon Post* (20-26 August) 3.

Atenga, Thomas Hirenée (1997) "SNES-France et SNAE en tournée: redynamiser les enseignants" *Le Messager* (3 mars), 9.

Baar, Carl (1989) "The Courts in Canada", in Jerold L. Waltman and Kenneth M. Holland (eds.), *The Political Role of Law Courts in Modern Democracies* (New York: St. Martin's Press), 53-82.

Barnett, R.E. (1987) "Judicial Pragmactivism: A Definition", in J.A. Dorn and H.G. Manne (eds.), *Economic Liberties and the Judiciary* (Fairfax: George Mason University Press), 205.

Baxi, Upendra (1987) "On the Shame of Not Being an Activist", in Neelan Tiruchelvam and Radhika Coomaraswamy (eds.), *The Judiciary in Plural Societies* (New York: St. Martin's Press), 168-78.

Bayefsky, Anne F. (1989) *Canada's Constitution Act 1982 and Amendments* Volume 1 (Toronto: McGraw-Hill Ryerson).

Beatty, David M. (1994) "Human Rights and the Rule of Law", in David M. Beatty (ed.), *Human Rights and Judicial Review – A Comparative Perspective* (Dordrecht: Martinus Nijhoff Publishers), 15-23.

Beaudoin, G. (1991) "La Cour suprême et le fédéralisme canadien", in Edmond Orban (ed.), *Fédéralisme et cours suprêmes/Federalism and Supreme Courts* (Bruxelles & Montréal: Établissement Émile Bruylant & Presses de l'Université de Montréal), 81.

Benjamin, Jacques (1972) *Les camerounais occidentaux: la minorité dans un état bicommunautaire* (Montréal: Université de Montréal).

Bernhart, Rudolf (1994) "Human Rights and Judicial Review: The European Court of Human Rights", in David M. Beatty (ed.), *Human Rights and Judicial Review – A Comparative Perspective* (Dordrecht: Martinus Nijhoff Publishers), 297.

Biya, Paul (1986) *Communal Liberalism* (London: Macmillan).

Bjornson, Richard (1991) *The African Quest for Freedom and Identity: Cameroonian Writing and the National Experience* (Bloomington & Indianapolis: Indiana University Press).

Bodo, Damien Fouda (1996) "Concours ou clientélisme?" *L'Effort Camerounais* (14-24 décembre), 6.

Bork, R. (1990) *The Tempting of America: The Political Seduction of the Law* (New York: Free Press).

Bothe, Michael (1991) "The Constitutional Court of the F.R.G. and the Powers of the Lander", in Edmond Orban (ed.), *Fédéralisme et cours suprêmes/Federalism and Supreme Courts* (Bruxelles & Montréal:

Établissement Émile Bruylant & Presses de l'Université de Montréal), 119.

Boyle, Patrick M. (1996) "Parents, Private Schools, and the Politics of an Emerging Civil Society in Cameroon" 34(4) *Journal of Modern African Studies* 609-22.

Bringer, Peter (1981) "The Abiding Influence of English and French Criminal Law in One African Country: Some Remarks Regarding the Machinery of Criminal Justice in Cameroon" 25(1) *Journal of African Law* 1-13.

Britannica (2002) *The New Encyclopaedia Britannica* Volume 4 (15th edition, Chicago: Encyclopaedia Britannica Inc.).

Brody, R. (1990) *Attacks on Justice: The Harassment and Persecution of Judges and Lawyers July 1989-June 1990* (Geneva: Centre for the Independence of Judges and Lawyers of the International Commission of Jurists).

Brodsky, Gwen and Shelagh Day (1989) *Canadian Charter Equality for Women: One Step Forward or Two Steps*

Back? (Ottawa: Canadian Advisory Council on the Status of Women).

Brownstein, Ronald (1998) "Exploding Impeachment Myths: Committee Deliberations Cleared Smoke Surrounding Lewinsky Affair" *Montreal Gazette* (15 December), B3.

Cairns, Alan C. (1990) "A Tribute to Donald V. Smiley", in Ronald L. Watts and Douglas M. Brown (eds.), *Canada: The State of the Federation 1990*(Kingston, Ontario: Institute of Intergovernmental Relations), viii.

Canadian Institute for the Administration of Justice, (1981)) *Compendium of Information on the Status and Role of the Chief Justice in Canada* (Montréal: International Centre for Comparative Criminology, Université de Montréal, October).

Cappelletti, M. (1991) *Judicial Review in the Contemporary World* (New York: The Bobbs-Merrill Company Inc.).

CBA-CBC Report (1989) *The Canadian Bar Association and the Cameroon Bar Council Committee Report:*

Model Human Rights Charter for Developing Countries 1989 (Ottawa: Canadian Bar Association).

Cheli, Enzo and Filippo Donati, (1994) "Methods and Criteria of Judgement on the Question of Rights to Freedom in Italy", in David M. Beatty (ed.), *Human Rights and Judicial Review – A Comparative Perspective* (Dordrecht: Martinus Nijhoff Publishers), 227.

Chen, SST (1971) *Theory and Practice of International Organization* (New York: MSS Education Publishing Co. Inc.).

Cohen, (1977) *Due Process of Law: The Canadian System of Justice* (Toronto: Carswell Co.).

Coomaraswamy, Radhika (1987) "Toward an Engaged Judiciary", in Neelan Tiruchelvam and Radhika Coomaraswamy (eds.), *The Judiciary in Plural Societies* (New York: St. Martin's Press), 1.

Day, F.D. (1964) *Criminal Law and Society* (Springfield, Illinois: C.C. Thomas).

Defeis, Elizabeth F. (1992) "Freedom of Speech and International Norms: Response to Hate Speech" 29 *Stanford Journal of International Law* 57.

Delpérée, F. (1991) "La Cour d'arbitrage et le fédéralisme belge", in Edmond Orban (ed.), *Fédéralisme et cours suprêmes/Federalism and Supreme Courts* (Bruxelles & Montréal: Établissement Émile Bruylant & Presses de l'Université de Montréal), 167.

Dempsey, Paul Stephen (2004) "Compliance and Enforcement in International Law: Achieving Global Uniformity in Aviation Safety" 30(1) *North Carolina Journal of International Law and Commercial Regulation* 1-74.

Denning, A.T. (1980) *Due Process of Law* (London: Butterworth).

_____ (1955) *The Road to Justice* (London: Stevens & Sons Ltd.).

_____ (1949) *Freedom under the Law* (London: Stevens and Sons).

Deschenes, Honourable Jules (1974) "Le rôle législatif du pouvoir judiciaire" (Address to the Chamber of Commerce of Montreal, 29 October).

Dicklitch, Susan (2002) "Failed Democratic Transition in Cameroon: A Human Rights Explanation" 24(1) *Human Rights Quarterly* 152-76.

Dickson, Chief Justice Brian (1985) "The Rule of Law: Judicial Independence and the Separation of Powers" (Address to the Canadian Bar Association, 21 August).

Dimond, P.R. (1989) *The Supreme Court and Judicial Choice* (Ann Arbor: The University of Michigan Press).

Dinga, J.S (1997) "What Cameroon for the Future?" *The Herald* (Yaoundé, 30 June -1 July), 4.

Dinstein, Yorman (1989) "Opening Remarks" 21(3) *New York University Journal of International Law and Politics* 451.

Diplock, Lord Kenneth (1964) "The Courts as Legislators" (Address to the Holdsworth Club of the University of Birmingham).

Dwomoh, Richard (2015) *The International Community and the Responsibility to Protect* (Germany: LAP Lambert Academic Publishers).

Dworkin, Ronald (1989) *Law's Empire* (Cambridge, Mass: Harvard University Press).

Ely, J. (1986) *Democracy and Distrust: A Theory of Judicial Review* (Cambridge, Mass: Harvard University Press).

Enonchong, H.N.A. (1967) *Cameroon Constitutional Law – Federalism in a Mixed Common-Law and Civil-Law System* (Yaoundé: Centre d'Édition et de Production de Manuel et d'Auxilliares de l'Enseignement).

Enonchong, Laura-Stella Eposi (2012) "Judicial Independence and Accountability in Cameroon: Balancing a Tenuous Relationship" 5(3) *African Journal of Legal Studies* 313-37.

Etahoben, Chief B. (1990) "Mrs Ebai Beats the Crisis Challenge, Quits Bench for Private Practice" *Cameroon Post* (July 31-August), 4.

Ewang, Andrew Sone (1997) "Can the Prosecutor Discontinue a Private Prosecution by Entering a *Nolle Prosequi?*" 31 *Juridis Péridique* 39.

_____ (1996) "The Cameroon Supreme Court: A Court of Judicial Review or a Cour de Cassation?" 25 *Juridis Périodique* 31-33.

Eyinga, Abel (1996) "Le régime néocolonial actuel a atteint un autre niveau dans la lutte contre la conscience nationale" *La Nouvelle Expression* N⁰ 338 (Douala, 30 août), 6-7.

Eyoh, Dickson (1998) "Conflicting Narratives of Anglophone Protest and the Politics of Identity in Cameroon" 16(2) *Journal of Contemporary African Studies* 249-76.

Favoreau, Louis (1991) "Preface" to Edmond Orban (ed.), *Fédéralisme et cours suprêmes/Federalism and Supreme Courts* (Bruxelles & Montréal: Établissement Émile Bruylant & Presses de l'Université de Montréal), 5-9.

Flanz, Gisbert H. (1994) "Germany", in Albert P. Blaustein and Gisbert H. Flanz (eds.), *Constitutions of the Countries of the World* (New York: Oceana Publications & Dobbs Ferry).

Fohtung, Barry B, (1996) "Yaounde or the ACME of Anglophone Masturbation-I" *Cameroon Post* Nº 0028 (8-14 October 1996), 8.

Fombad, Charles Manga (2014) "Strengthening Constitutional Order and Upholding the Rule of Law in Central Africa: Reversing the Descent towards Symbolic Constitutionalism" 14 *African Human Rights Law Journal* 412-48.

_____ (1998) "The New Cameroonian Constitutional Council in a Comparative Perspective: Progress or Retrogression?" 42 *Journal of African Law* 172-86.

Fossungu, Peter Ateh-Afac (2018a) "Political Naivety, Corruption, and Poverty Promotion in Africa: Riding the 'Poorest-ugliest French' Bijuralism Horse from Cameroon to Canada via Britain", in Munyaradzi Mawere (ed.), *The Political Economy of Poverty,*

Vulnerability and Disaster Risk Management: Building Bridges of Resilience, Entrepreneurship and Development in Africa's 21st Century (Bamenda: Langaa RPCIG) 123-73.

_____ (2018b) *Historical and Partyological Postponement of Democracy in Canada: Elongating the Business Pleasure War in Africa?* (Germany: LAP Lambert Academic Publishers).

_____ (2016) "Afrikenticating and Revisiting the Anglophone Lawyers' Imbroglio in Cameroon" @ http://cameroonjournal.com/national-news/opinion-afrikenticating-and-revisiting-the-anglophone-lawyers-imbroglio-in-cameroon/ (last accessed on 21 April 2017).

_____ (2015a) *The HISOFE Dictionary of Midnight Politics: Expibasketical Theories on Afrikentication and African Unity* (Bamenda: Langaa RPCIG).

_____ (2015b) "African Democracy vis-a-vis Western Democracy: Afrikenticating, Follyfying, Expibasketizing, and Reversing the 'African

Democracy' Debate", in Munyaradzi Mawere and Tendal Rinos Mwanaka (eds.), *Democracy, Good Governance and Development in Africa* (Bamenda: Langaa RPCIG), 71-124.

_____ (2015c) *Family Politics and Deception in Northern North America and West-Central Africa: Litigating God's Marriage Intention?* (Bamenda: Langaa RPCIG).

_____ (2013a) *Understanding Confusion in Africa: The Politics of Multiculturalism and Nation-building in Cameroon* (Bamenda: Langaa RPCIG).

_____ (2013b) *Democracy and Human Rights in Africa: The Politics of Collective Participation and Governance in Cameroon* (Bamenda: Langaa RPCIG).

_____ (2013c) *Africans in Canada: Blending Canadian and African Lifestyles?* (Bamenda: Langaa RPCIG).

_____ (1999a) "The Oppressive Policing Role of Courts in Cameroon" *The Herald* (Yaoundé, 15-17 January), 10.

_____ (1999b) "999 University, Please Help the Third World (Africa) Help Itself: A Critique of Council Elections" (1999) 64 *Journal of Air Law and Commerce* 339-75.

_____ (1998a) "Revisiting 'My Second Home'" *The Herald* (Yaoundé, 26-27 August), 10.

_____ (1998b) "The Constitutional Council and the Ropeless Lilliputians" *The Herald* Nº 682 (Yaoundé, 4-5 November), 4.

_____ (1998c) "The Convicts and the Prison Guard" *The Herald* (Yaoundé, 3-5 April), 10.

_____ (1998d) "On the Lack of Academic Journals in Cameroon: Salute to *Juridis Périodique*" *The Herald* (Yaoundé, 27-28 May 1998), 4.

_____ (1998e) "Many Constitutions Create Confusion" *The Herald* (Yaoundé, 4-6 December), 4.

_____ (1997) "Sentencing Criminals in Cameroon: Tying Judges' Hands and Expecting Them to Do Gymnastics?" (1997) 29 *Juridis Périodique* (*Revue de Droit et de Science Politique*) 84-98.

Freedman, M.D.A. (1994) *Lloyd's Introduction to Jurisprudence* (6th edition, London: Sweet and Maxwell Ltd.).

Freeman, Alan (1982) "Anti-Discrimination Law: A Critical Review" in David Kairys (ed.), *The Politics of Law: A Progressive Critique* (New York: Pantheon Books, 1982), 96.

Frye, Northrop (1986) "Language as the Home of Human Life" in Michael Owen (ed.), *Salute to Scholarship: Essays Presented at the Official Opening of Athabasca University* (Athabasca: Athabasca University), 20-33.

Gibson, Dale (1987) "Judges as Legislators: Not Whether But How" 25(2) *Alberta Law Review* 249.

Goell, Yosef Israel (1978) *Bi-Nationalism and Bi-Lingualism in Three Modernized States: A Comparative Study of Canada, Belgium, and White South Africa* (PhD Dissertation, Columbia University, University Microfilms International).

Green, L. (1986) "Book Review of *The Rule of Law: Ideal or Ideology* by Alan C. Hutchinson and P. Monahan" 24 *Osgoode Hall Law Journal* 1023.

Gwyn, W.B. (1965) *The Meaning of Separation of Powers: An Analysis of the Doctrine from its Origin to the Adoption of the United States Constitution* (The Hague: Martinus Nijhoff).

Havilland, H.F. (1978) *The Political Role of the General Assembly* (Westport, CT: Greenwood Press Inc.).

Hodgins, Bruce W., John J. Eddy, Shelagh D. Grant and James Struthers (eds.), (1989) *Federalism in Canada and Australia: Historical Perspectives, 1920-1988* (Peterborough, Ontario: Frost Centre for Canadian Heritage and Development Studies).

Hogg, Peter W. (1996) *Constitutional Law of Canada* (4th Student edition, Toronto: Thomson Canada Limited).

Holland, Kenneth M. (1989) "The Courts in the United States" in Jerold L. Waltman and Kenneth M. Holland (eds.), *The Political Role of Law Courts in Modern Democracies* (New York: St. Martin's Press), 6-30.

Hutchinson, Alan C. (1995) "Calgary and Everything After: A Postmodern Re-Vision of Lawyering" 33(4) *Alberta Law Review* 768.

Iacobucci, Frank (1994) "Judicial Review by the Supreme Court of Canada under the Charter of Rights and Freedoms: The First Ten Years", in David. M. Beatty (ed.), *Human Rights and Judicial Review – A Comparative Perspective* (Dordrecht: Martinus Nijhoff Publishers), 93-134.

Ikeda, Daisaku (1987) *A Lasting Peace* Vol. II (New York & Tokyo: Weatherhill).

Johnson, Willard R. (1970) *The Cameroon Federation: Political Integration in a Fragmentary Society* (Princeton, N.J.: Princeton University Press).

Jumbam, Fr. Gerald (2017) "An Open Letter to the President of the National Episcopal Conference of Cameroon (NECC) – Archbishop Samuel Kleda" (Letter obtained on 8 May 2017 at 12:11 PM from Oben Besong who sent it to the Soba-America Forum) (on File with author).

Katz, Elllis (1991) "The U.S. Supreme Court and the Integration of American Federalism" in Edmond Orban (ed.), *Fédéralisme et cours suprêmes/Federalism and Supreme Courts* (Bruxelles & Montréal: Établissement Émile Bruylant & Presses de l'Université de Montréal), 35.

Keating, M. (1986) *Decentralization and Change in Contemporary France* (Brookfield, Vermont: Gower Publishing Company).

Kentridge, Catherine (1995) "Dilemmas" *Canadian Lawyer* (January), 4.

Kfua, Bonny (1996) "France, Democratise Cameroon" *The Herald* (Yaoundé, 7-8 October) 4.

Kidane, René (1997) "Apres les avantages accordés aux magistrats, les enseignants du 'supérieure' exigent leur part" *Le Messager* (3 mars), 9.

Kirkpatrick, J.J. (1983) *Dictatorships and Double Standards: Rationalism and Reason in Politics*, as reviewed in 15(2) *New York University Journal of International Law & Politics* 743.

Klots, A.T (1973) "The Selection of Judges and the Short Ballot" in G.R. Winters (ed.), *Judicial Selection and Tenure* (rev. ed., Chicago: American Judicature Society), 78.

Kneier, Charles M. (1939) *Illustrative Materials in Municipal Government and Administration* (1st edition, New York: Harper & Brothers).

Laski, Harold-J. (1950) *Le gouvernement parlementaire en Angleterre* (Trans. J. Cadart and J. Prélot) (Paris: P.U.F.).

Lokan, Andrew (1992) "The Rise and Fall of the Doctrine under Section 1 of the Charter" 24 *Ottawa Law Review* 163.

Lord Hailsham of Marylebone, (1989) "The Separation of Powers and the Office of the Lord Chancellor" 8 *Civil Justice Quarterly* 308.

Loewenstein, Karl (1967) *British Cabinet Government* (London: Oxford University Press).

Mallory, J.R. (1984) *The Structure of Canadian Government* (Toronto: Gage Publishing Company).

Mandel, Michael (1989) *The Charter of Rights and the Legalization of Politics in Canada* (Toronto: Wall and Thompson).

Maneli, Mieczyslaw (1994) *Perelman's New Rhetoric as Philosophy and Methodology for the Next Century* (Dordrecht: Kluwer Academic Publishers).

Matsuda, Mari J. (1989) "Public Response to Racist Speech: Considering the Victim's Story" 87 *Michigan Law Review* 2320.

Mbaku, John Mukum (2018) *Protecting Minority Rights in African Countries: A Constitutional Political Economy Approach* (Cheltenham, UK: Edward Elgar Publishing Ltd.).

_____ (2014) "Judicial Independence, Constitutionalism and Governance in Cameroon: Lessons from French Constitutional Practice" 1(4) *European Journal of Comparative Law and Governance* 357-91.

_____ (2014b) The Rule of Law and Poverty Eradication in Africa" 13(4) *African and Asian Studies* 530-57.

Mbuagbo, Oben Timothy (2002) "Cameroon: Exploiting Anglophone Identity in State Deconstruction" 8(3) *Social Identities* 431-38.

McWhinney, Edwards (1982) *Canada and the Constitution 1979-1982: Patriation and the Charter of Rights* (Toronto: University of Toronto Press).

Mehier, Andreas (2014) "Why Federalism Did Not Lead to Secession in Cameroon" 13(1) *Ethnopolitics* 48-66.

Mensah-Gbadago, M.M. (1991) "9 Years of Political Transition: From Ahidjo to Biya and the Hayatou Connection – How Far Have We Moved?" *Le Messager* Special Political Issue (Yaoundé, 6 June) 1.

Mentan, Tatah (2017) "Shaming Heaven: Peace of the Graveyard in Cameroon" @ http://cameroonjournal.com/2017/04/11/comment ary-shaming-heaven-peace-of-the-graveyard-in-cameroon/.

Mhango, Nkwazi Nkuzi (2018) *How Africa Developed Europe: Deconstructing the His-story of Africa, Excavating Untold Truth and What Ought to Be Done and Known* (Bamenda: Langaa RPCIG).

Ndi Chia, Charly (1995) "We May Not Be the World But We Are the People" *Cameroon Post* (11-18 December), 4.

Ndifor, Asong (1996) "Fru Ndi Tells France to Advise Biya" *The Herald* (Yaoundé, 13-15 May), 1.

Ngwafor, Aldarin (1998) "Urgent Need for a Law School in Cameroon" *The Herald* (Yaoundé, 12-14 June), 4.

Nicholas, Herbert George (1963) *The United Nations as a Political Institution* (2nd edition, New York: Oxford University Press).

Nkengasong, John Nkemngong (2012) "Interrogating the Union: Anglophone Cameroon Poetry in the Postcolonial Matrix" 48(1) *Journal of Postcolonial Writing* 51-64.

Nyo'Wakai (1991) "Former Judge Nyo'Wakai Talks to the Messager on the Cameroonian Judicial System" *Le*

Messager Special Political Issue (Yaoundé, Thursday 6 June), 18-19.

_____ (1989) "Foreword II" to Carlson Anyangwe, *The Magistracy and the Bar in Cameroon* (Yaoundé: PANAG-CEPER).

Ofege, Ntemfac (1995) "Constitutional Revision: Vistas of Anglophone Exclusion and Presidential Hypocrisy" *Cameroon Post* № 0274 (11-18 December), 8.

Olugbuo, Benson Chinedu (2014) "The African Union, the United Nations Security Council and the Politicisation of International Justice in Africa" 7(3) *African Journal of Legal Studies* 351-79.

Ondoa, Magloire (1996) "Commentaire" 25 *Juridis Périodique* (*Revue de Droit et de Science Politique*) 11-14.

Orban, Edmond (1991) "La Cour constitutionnelle fédérale et l'autonomie des Lander en R.F.A.", in Edmond Orban (ed.), *Fédéralisme et cours suprêmes/Federalism and Supreme Courts* (Bruxelles

& Montréal: Établissement Émile Bruylant & Presses de l'Université de Montréal), 137.

Orock, Rogers Tabe Egbe and Oben Timothy Mbuagbo, (2012) "'Why Government Should Not Collect Taxes': Grand Corruption in Government and Citizens` Views on Taxation in Cameroon" 39(233) *Review of African Political Economy* 479-99.

Osofisan, Femi (1996) "Warriors of a Failed Utopia? – West African Writers Since the '70s" (being lecture delivered at The Second Annual African Studies Lecture given at the University of Leeds on the 24th April 1996) 61 *Leeds African Studies Bulletin* 11.

Parker, Graham (1986) "Canadian Criminal Law", in Robert A. Silverman and James J. Teevan (eds.), *Crime in Canadian Society* (Toronto: Butterworth,), 14-40.

Pasquet, D. (1968) "The Representatives as Tools of an Aspiring Autocrat", in G.P. Bodet (ed.), *Early English Parliaments: High Courts, Royal Councils, or Representative Assemblies?*(Boston: D.C. Heath and Company), 46.

Radamaker, Dallis (1987) "The Courts in France", in Jerold L. Waltman and Kenneth M. Holland (eds.), *The Political Role of Law Courts in Modern Democracies* (New York: St. Martin's Press), 129-152.

Reno, Janet (1994) "Remarks: Address Delivered at the Celebration of the Seventy-fifth Anniversary of Women at Fordham Law School" 63(1) *Fordham Law Review* 5-15.

Rodino, Peter W. (1990) "Living with the Preamble" 42 *Rutgers Law Review* 685.

Rubington, Earl and Martin S. Weinberg 1981) "Social Problems and Sociology", in Earl Rubington and Martin S. Weinberg (eds.), *The Study of Social Problems: Five Perspectives* (3rd edition, New York: Oxford University Press), 3-12.

Russell, Peter H. (1987) *The Judiciary in Canada: Third Branch of Government* (Toronto: McGraw-Hill Ryerson Ltd.).

_____ (1969) *The Supreme Court of Canada as a Bilingual and Bicultural Institution: Documents of the*

Royal Commission on Bilingualism and Biculturalism (Ottawa: Queen's Printer for Canada).

Schabas, William (1991) *International Human Rights Law and the Canadian Charter: A Manual for the Practitioner* (Toronto: Carswell).

Schmidt, V.A. (1990) *Democratizing France: The Political and Administrative History of Decentralization* (New York: Cambridge University Press).

Schneiderman, David (1992) "Introduction" in David Schneiderman (ed.), *Conversations Among Friends <<>> Amies: Proceedings of an Interdisciplinary Conference on Women and Constitutional Reform* (Edmonton: Centre for Constitutional Studies), 5.

Segaller, Stephen (1987) *Invisible Armies: Terrorism into the 1990s* (San Diego: Harcourt Brace Jovanovich).

Shapiro, Evan Joel (1995) *The Supranational Challenge: Federal and Decentralized Unitary States within the European Union* (LL.M. Thesis, Institute of Comparative Law, McGill University).

Sibafo, J.D. (1996) "Des questions et d'autres: la démocratie façon RDPC" *La Nouvelle Expression* (Yaoundé, 30 août), 9.

Shoalts, D. (1991) "Image Doesn't Do J-P.s Justice – Judicial Duties Go Far Beyond Civil Marriages" *Globe and Mail* (Toronto) (17 September 1991), A4.

Silverman, Robert A. and James J. Teevan, Jr. (1986) "Definition of Crime', in Robert A. Silverman and James J. Teevan (eds.), *Crime in Canadian Society* (Toronto: Butterworth), 1-13.

Smith, J.A. Clarence (1968) "The Cameroon Penal Code: Practical Comparative Law" 17 *International and Comparative Law Quarterly* 651.

Sochor, Eugene (1991) *The Politics of International Aviation* (Iowa City: University of Iowa Press).

Sonobe, Itsuo (1994) "Human Rights and Constitutional Review in Japan", in David M. Beatty (ed.), *Human Rights and Judicial Review – A Comparative Perspective* (Dordrecht: Martinus Nijhoff Publishers), 135.

Stark, Frank M. (1976) "Federalism in Cameroon: The Shadow and the Reality" 10(3) *Canadian Journal of African Studies* 423-42.

Stason, E.B. (1973) "Judicial Selection around the World", in Glenn R. Winters (ed.), *Judicial Selection and Tenure* (rev. ed., Chicago: American Judicature Society), 45.

Sunde, Lucas (1996) "Execution of Bad Laws: Anglophone Lawyers Told to Blame Assembly Not Supreme Court" *The Herald* (Yaoundé, 24-26 June), 3.

Takougang, Joseph (2003) "Nationalism, Democratisation and Political Opportunism in Cameroon" 21(3) *Journal of Contemporary African Studies* 427-45.

Tiruchelvam, Neelan (1987) "Introduction" in Neelan Tiruchelvam and Radhika Coomaraswamy (eds.), *The Judiciary in Plural Societies* (New York: St. Martin's Press), vii-xxi.

Tocqueville, Alexis de (1945) *Democracy in America* Volume I (New York: Alfred A. Knopf).

Totalé, Gervais Nitcheu (1996) "Barreau Assemblée générale des avocats: le tribalisme engendre la fraude" *L'Effort Camerounais* (24 décembre), 4.

Tremblay, André (1993) *Droit Constitutionnel: Principes* (Montréal: Les Éditions Thémis).

Turpel, Mary Ellen (1991) "Aboriginal Peoples and the Canadian Charter: Interpretive Monopolies, Cultural Differences", in RF Devlin (ed.), *Canadian Perspectives on Legal Theory* (Toronto: Emond Montgomery Publications Limited, 1991), 503-538.

Wade, H. W. R. (1980) *Constitutional Fundamentals* (London: Stevenson and Sons).

Waltman, Jerold L. (1989) "Introduction" in Jerold L. Waltman and Kenneth M. Holland (eds.), *The Political Role of Law Courts in Modern Democracies* (New York: St. Martin's Press), 1-5.

Wambali, M.B.K. and C.M. Peter (1987) "The Judiciary in Context: The Case of Tanzania", in Neelan Tiruchelvam and Radhika Coomaraswamy (eds.), *The Judiciary in Plural Societies* (New York: St. Martin's Press), 131.

Wellington, H. (1982) "The Nature of Judicial Review" 91 *Yale Law Journal* 486.

Wheare, K. C. (1963) *Federal Government* (London: Oxford University Press).

Williams, Patricia J. (1987) "Alchemical Notes: Reconstructing Ideals from Deconstructed Rights" 22 *Harvard Civil Rights-Civil Liberty Law Review* 401-433.

www.ingramcontent.com/pod-product-compliance
Lightning Source LLC
Chambersburg PA
CBHW050644280326
41932CB00015B/2779